I0519140

THE AUTONOMOUS WAVE. THE RISE AND IMPACT OF AUTONOMOUS SHIPS AND AUTONOMOUS SHIP MANAGEMENT COMPANIES

By: Mustafa Nejem

TABLE OF CONTENT

COPYRIGHT SECTION

This book, "The Autonomous Wave. The Rise and Impact of Autonomous Ships and Autonomous Ship Management Companies," is protected by copyright.

All rights, including the right to reproduce, distribute, or transmit any part of this work in any form, are reserved. No part of this book may be reproduced, stored, or transmitted in any form or by any means, including electronic, mechanical, photocopying, recording, or otherwise, without the prior written permission of the copyright owner.

For permissions and inquiries, please contact the publisher. Thank you for respecting the intellectual property rights of the author and publisher.

Chapter 1

INTRODUCTION

The maritime industry is on the brink of a profound transformation driven by technological innovation and automation. At the heart of this maritime revolution lies the advent of autonomous ships, a disruptive force poised to redefine how we navigate and manage vessels on the open seas. This chapter sets the stage for exploring this remarkable phenomenon, delving into the definitions, key players, and overarching trends underpinning the autonomous wave.

DEFINITION OF AUTONOMOUS SHIPS

Autonomous ships represent a revolutionary evolution within the maritime industry, redefining how vessels navigate and operate on the world's oceans. At their core, autonomous ships are maritime vessels capable of performing a wide range of tasks, functions, and operations with a high degree of autonomy, reducing or eliminating the need for direct human intervention. This autonomy is made possible by integrating cutting-edge technologies and sophisticated systems, including artificial intelligence, machine learning, advanced sensors, satellite navigation, high-performance computing, and control systems.

KEY CHARACTERISTICS OF AUTONOMOUS SHIPS.

1. Independence. Autonomous ships can operate independently, making decisions and executing tasks without continuous human oversight. They can navigate routes, avoid obstacles, respond to changing environmental conditions, and even conduct emergency procedures autonomously.

2. Real-time Data Processing. These vessels have advanced sensors and AI-driven systems that continuously collect, process and analyse real-time data from their surroundings. This data is used to make informed decisions, optimise routes, and ensure safe navigation.

3. Levels of Autonomy. Autonomous ships exist on a spectrum of autonomy, ranging from vessels that humans remotely control to fully autonomous ships that operate entirely without human intervention. The level of autonomy is determined by the vessel's design, technology, and operational requirements.

4. Adaptive Learning. Machine learning algorithms are integral to autonomous ships, enabling them to adapt and improve their performance over time. They can learn from past experiences, adjust to changing conditions, and enhance their decision-making capabilities.

5. Safety Mechanisms. Safety is paramount in autonomous shipping. These vessels have robust safety protocols, fail-safe mechanisms, and redundancy systems to ensure safe operations and mitigate risks.

6. Integration of Technologies. Autonomous ships integrate many technologies, including satellite navigation for precise positioning, advanced sensors to perceive their environment (e.g., radar, lidar, cameras), and high-performance computing for rapid data processing.

7. Remote Monitoring. Many autonomous ships can be monitored and controlled remotely from onshore control centres, allowing experts to oversee operations, intervene when necessary, and support the vessel.

8. Compliance and Regulations. As autonomous shipping evolves, it must adhere to international and regional safety, security, environmental protection, and navigation regulations.

These vessels can potentially revolutionise the maritime industry by offering increased safety, enhanced operational efficiency, reduced labour costs, greater flexibility in logistics, and even environmental benefits. However, their adoption also presents significant challenges, including addressing legal and regulatory frameworks, cybersecurity concerns, trust-building with stakeholders, liability considerations, and effective communication and collaboration within the maritime ecosystem. As we delve deeper into the world of autonomous ships, it becomes evident that these vessels represent a technological advancement and a transformative force in the maritime landscape.

ROLE OF AUTONOMOUS SHIP MANAGEMENT COMPANIES

Autonomous Ship Management Companies are pivotal entities in the rapidly evolving world of maritime transportation. As the maritime industry embraces the era of autonomous ships, these specialised companies play a multifaceted role in ensuring the seamless operation, maintenance, and management of these advanced vessels. Their contributions encompass a wide array of services and responsibilities.

REMOTE MONITORING AND CONTROL CENTRES

One of the central functions of Autonomous Ship Management Companies is establishing and operating remote monitoring and control centres. These centres serve as the nerve centre for overseeing the performance of autonomous ships. They are equipped with advanced monitoring systems, enabling experts to track vessel movements, monitor environmental conditions, and intervene when necessary, ensuring safe and efficient navigation.

REMOTE DIAGNOSTICS AND MAINTENANCE

Autonomous Ship Management Companies employ cutting-edge technologies for remote diagnostics and maintenance. Through real-time data transmission and analysis, they can identify technical issues, troubleshoot, and perform software updates or repairs from onshore locations. This minimises downtime and reduces the need for physical inspections.

SYSTEM INTEGRATION AND OPTIMIZATION

These companies are responsible for the seamless integration and optimisation of the myriad systems on autonomous ships. This includes ensuring that navigation, communication, propulsion, and safety systems work cohesively to achieve the vessel's objectives efficiently and safely.

DATA ANALYTICS FOR PERFORMANCE ANALYSIS

Data is a valuable asset in autonomous shipping. These companies utilise advanced data analytics tools to process and analyse vast amounts of data generated during ship operations. This data-driven approach allows for performance analysis, route optimisation, predictive maintenance, and the enhancement of overall operational efficiency.

CREW TRAINING FOR TRANSITION

Autonomous Ship Management Companies offer specialised training programs for maritime crews to adapt to the new era of autonomous vessels. This includes training on onboard technology, understanding the role of autonomous systems, and preparing crew members to operate and manage these ships effectively.

UTILISING AI AND NEW TECHNOLOGIES

These companies harness the power of artificial intelligence (AI) and emerging technologies to improve the management and operation of autonomous vessels continually. AI-driven algorithms enable predictive maintenance, advanced route planning, and real-time decision-making, enhancing safety and efficiency.

SAFETY AND EMERGENCY PROTOCOLS

Autonomous Ship Management Companies are deeply committed to safety. They establish and enforce rigorous safety protocols, including emergency response plans and fail-safe mechanisms, to ensure that autonomous ships can respond effectively to unforeseen circumstances or emergencies.

REGULATORY COMPLIANCE

In a complex regulatory landscape, these companies navigate the intricacies of international and regional maritime regulations to ensure that autonomous ships comply with safety, security, environmental, and navigation standards. They collaborate with regulatory authorities to facilitate the integration of autonomous vessels into existing frameworks.

RESEARCH AND DEVELOPMENT

Autonomous Ship Management Companies engage in ongoing research initiatives and technological advancements to stay at the forefront of the industry. They invest in innovation to develop and implement new technologies that enhance the capabilities and safety of autonomous ships.

GLOBAL COLLABORATION

In an increasingly interconnected world, these companies foster international collaboration within the maritime industry. They participate in research and development collaborations, share best practices, and contribute to developing standardised approaches for autonomous shipping on a global scale.

Autonomous Ship Management Companies act as the linchpin between cutting-edge technology and the practical application of autonomous vessels in maritime operations. Their expertise, services, and commitment to safety are instrumental in shaping the future of autonomous shipping, making it safer, more efficient, and environmentally sustainable. As autonomous ships continue to navigate the seas of change, these companies are at the forefront, steering the industry towards a new era of maritime transportation.

OVERVIEW OF THE GROWING TREND

The maritime industry is witnessing a profound transformation driven by the inexorable rise of autonomous ships. This burgeoning trend is propelled by a convergence of technological advancements, economic imperatives, and environmental considerations. With their ability to operate independently and efficiently, autonomous ships are poised to redefine how goods are transported across the world's oceans. The allure of increased safety, enhanced operational efficiency, reduced labour costs, and flexibility in hazardous and remote operations has spurred widespread interest in this transformative technology.

However, the adoption of autonomous shipping is not without its challenges. The complex and ever-evolving legal and regulatory frameworks present hurdles that must be navigated. Cybersecurity concerns loom as these vessels become more digitally connected, and trust-building with stakeholders becomes paramount. Moreover, considerations related to liability, insurance, and effective communication and collaboration within the maritime ecosystem must be addressed.

Nonetheless, the promise of the autonomous wave is too compelling to ignore. As more companies invest in research and development and regulatory authorities adapt to the changing landscape, the adoption of autonomous ships is expected to grow. This growing trend has far-reaching implications, from evolving maritime jobs and skillsets to environmental benefits and sustainability considerations.

In this book, we will delve deep into the heart of this burgeoning trend, exploring the technologies that underpin it, the key players shaping its trajectory, and the impacts that extend beyond the confines of the maritime industry.

As we delve deeper into the chapters of this book, we will also explore the technologies driving autonomous ships, the roles of Autonomous Ship Management Companies, the impacts on the maritime industry, future trends, safety considerations, and much more.

The growing trend towards autonomy in maritime transportation is not just a fleeting wave; it is a tidal shift that will reshape the seascape of the global maritime industry for years to come.

Chapter 2

AUTONOMOUS SHIPS

In the maritime industry's relentless pursuit of innovation, autonomous ships stand at the forefront of technological advancement. These vessels, equipped with cutting-edge technologies, represent a pivotal shift in how we conceive, design, and operate maritime transportation.

This chapter embarks on a deep and updated exploration of autonomous ships, dissecting the intricate web of technologies that power them, the transformative benefits they offer, and the complex challenges they confront.

TECHNOLOGIES SHAPING AUTONOMOUS SHIPS

1. ADVANCED SENSORS

Autonomous ships have revolutionised the maritime industry by deploying a sophisticated network of sensors that mimic and even surpass human perception. These cutting-edge sensors include radar systems utilising radio waves to detect distant vessels and potential hazards. Lidar, a laser-based technology, creates precise 3D maps of the ship's environment, allowing it to navigate through complex scenarios with remarkable precision. Sonar systems, inspired by the echolocation abilities of marine creatures, provide underwater depth perception and help avoid underwater obstacles. Additionally, an array of high-resolution cameras captures visual data, enhancing the ship's situational awareness.

These sensors collaborate seamlessly to provide a constant stream of real-time data. The sensors empower autonomous ships to make split-second decisions by identifying nearby vessels and tracking their movements to assess changing weather conditions. This level of awareness rivals and, in many cases, surpasses the capabilities of human captains, ensuring safe and efficient navigation on the high seas.

2. SATELLITE NAVIGATION

The heart of autonomous ship navigation lies in using advanced satellite systems, most notably the Global Positioning System (GPS). With unparalleled precision, GPS satellites orbiting high above the Earth beam signals down to autonomous ships below. These signals contain precise timing information that allows the ship's onboard receivers to calculate their exact position on the planet's surface.

Using satellite navigation empowers autonomous ships to chart courses with incredible accuracy, ensuring they reach their destinations efficiently and safely. The ships can dynamically adjust their routes to avoid obstacles, whether other vessels, icebergs, or treacherous underwater terrain. Furthermore, maintaining position with pinpoint accuracy is crucial in scenarios like offshore drilling or scientific research, where precise station-keeping is essential.

In addition to GPS, other global navigation satellite systems, such as GLONASS and Galileo, contribute to the redundancy and robustness of these systems, enhancing the reliability of autonomous ship navigation. These satellite systems have transformed the maritime landscape, ushering in a new era of safe, efficient, and precise ship navigation on a global scale.

3. HIGH-PERFORMANCE COMPUTING

At the core of autonomous ships lies the computational powerhouse known as high-performance computing (HPC) systems. These HPC systems serve as the digital brain of the vessel, tirelessly processing the immense volumes of data generated by the myriad of sensors and navigation systems onboard. This computational prowess is the linchpin of autonomous operations, enabling the ship to make rapid and well-informed decisions while simultaneously maximising operational efficiency.

These HPC systems analyse sensor data in real time, rapidly crunching numbers and sifting through information. They play a pivotal role in assessing the ship's surroundings, identifying potential hazards, and executing navigation strategies that keep the vessel and its crew, if any, out of harm's way. Moreover, these systems provide the foundation for autonomous ships to operate in diverse and dynamic environments, ensuring they can adapt to unexpected challenges with unparalleled speed and accuracy.

4. AI AND NEW TECHNOLOGIES

Artificial Intelligence (AI) is the beating heart of autonomy in these maritime marvels. Machine learning algorithms, a subset of AI, are the key to granting autonomous ships the ability to learn from past experiences, adapt to evolving circumstances, and make decisions that optimise safety and efficiency.

Through continuous data analysis, these AI systems build a repository of knowledge that grows with each voyage. They become adept at recognising patterns in sensor data, allowing the ship to anticipate potential issues and respond proactively. Moreover, AI-driven decision-making ensures that every action is tailored to the specific context, from adjusting course to maximise fuel efficiency to fine-tuning sensor configurations to adapt to varying weather conditions.

The integration of new technologies, such as computer vision and natural language processing, further augments the capabilities of autonomous ships. These technologies enable vessels to "see" and "understand" their surroundings and communicate and collaborate with ships, port facilities, and even humans onshore. In essence, AI and emerging technologies serve as the dynamic intelligence that empowers autonomous ships to navigate the complexities of the maritime world with unmatched skill and efficiency.

5. EMERGING TECHNOLOGIES

As the world of autonomous shipping continues to evolve, it remains poised to embrace various cutting-edge technologies, adapting to the ever-changing landscape of innovation. One of the potential game-changers on the horizon is blockchain technology. The integration of blockchain could revolutionise data sharing within the maritime industry. By leveraging blockchain's immutable and secure nature, autonomous ships can ensure the integrity and confidentiality of critical data. This includes data related to cargo manifests, vessel positions, and environmental conditions. With blockchain, sensitive information can be securely shared with stakeholders such as port authorities, customs officials, and shipping partners, fostering transparency and trust in the global maritime ecosystem.

Another pivotal advancement is the advent of 5G connectivity. The implementation of 5G networks opens up a world of possibilities for real-time communication and data exchange. Autonomous ships with 5G connectivity can maintain constant, high-speed connections with remote monitoring centres, fellow vessels, and coastal infrastructure. This capability enhances communication efficiency and supports the rapid transfer of critical navigational data and updates. Moreover, it enables seamless collaboration between autonomous ships, allowing them to work cohesively in congested waterways or during complex operations. The integration of 5G technology is poised to usher in a new era of connectivity, propelling autonomous ships into unprecedented responsiveness and adaptability.

6. PREDICTIVE ANALYTICS

The deployment of predictive analytics algorithms represents a transformative leap forward in the capabilities of autonomous ships. These algorithms harness the power of data and sophisticated mathematical models to peer into the future, allowing these vessels to anticipate many critical factors that impact their operations.

One of the most compelling applications of predictive analytics lies in weather forecasting. Autonomous ships can make highly accurate predictions about upcoming weather patterns by analysing historical weather data, current atmospheric conditions, and other relevant factors. This foresight enables them to proactively adjust their routes to avoid storms, heavy seas, or adverse weather conditions, ensuring not only the safety of the vessel but also the protection of valuable cargo and the well-being of onboard personnel.

Furthermore, predictive analytics extends its reach to monitor and predict sea state changes. By continuously assessing data from onboard sensors and external sources, these algorithms can anticipate shifts in sea conditions. This capability is instrumental in optimising the ship's speed and course, minimising the impact of rough seas on fuel consumption and voyage duration.

Moreover, predictive analytics algorithms can delve into the performance metrics of the vessel itself. They analyse engine efficiency, fuel consumption patterns, and wear and tear on critical components. With this information, autonomous ships can predict when maintenance is required, helping to prevent breakdowns and costly downtime.

7. IoT CONNECTIVITY

The seamless integration of the Internet of Things (IoT) into autonomous ships marks a groundbreaking advancement in maritime technology. IoT sensors and devices have become indispensable components, constantly monitoring the health and performance of critical ship systems. These sensors are deployed throughout the vessel, from the engine room to the cargo hold, collecting a wealth of data.

In the engine room, IoT sensors diligently track engine performance, ensuring optimal efficiency and alerting operators to any anomalies or signs of wear and tear. Machinery conditions are continuously assessed, allowing for proactive maintenance to prevent costly breakdowns and minimise downtime. Fuel consumption is closely monitored, contributing to efficient resource management and reduced environmental impact.

The real-time data these IoT devices collect is transmitted to onboard control systems, where sophisticated algorithms analyse it. This data-driven approach empowers autonomous ships to make informed decisions, such as adjusting engine settings for fuel efficiency or alerting crew members to potential maintenance needs. As a result, these vessels operate with unprecedented reliability, cost-effectiveness, and safety, setting new standards for the maritime industry.

8.   AUTONOMOUS ROBOTICS

Innovations in autonomous shipping extend beyond data analytics to physical capabilities, with some vessels now featuring onboard robotic systems. These autonomous robots serve various functions, from handling cargo to performing offshore operations and conducting environmental monitoring.

Cargo handling robots efficiently load and unload containers, crates, and goods, streamlining the logistics process and minimising the need for manual labour. Offshore operations benefit from robotic precision, with these machines carrying out tasks such as maintenance and repairs on underwater structures or subsea exploration with dexterity and accuracy surpassing human capabilities.

Environmental monitoring is another area where autonomous ships shine. Equipped with specialised robotic sensors and probes, these vessels can collect vital data about ocean conditions, water quality, and marine life. This data is invaluable for scientific research and environmental conservation efforts.

These autonomous robotic extensions enhance the operational capabilities of ships, making them versatile and adaptable to a wide range of tasks. They increase efficiency and contribute to safety by reducing the need for humans to perform dangerous or repetitive tasks in challenging maritime environments. As a result, autonomous ships equipped with robotics are at the forefront of innovation, changing how we think about maritime operations.

9.   HYDRODYNAMIC DESIGN

The hydrodynamic design of autonomous ships represents a fusion of art and science, where engineering excellence meets environmental consciousness. These vessels boast advanced hull shapes and propulsion systems meticulously crafted to glide through the water with minimal resistance, maximising fuel efficiency and their environmental footprint.

The hulls of these ships are the result of extensive research and computational simulations. They are designed to minimise drag and wave resistance, allowing the vessel to slice through the water easily. The hull's shape often optimised through computational fluid dynamics, ensures that the ship moves efficiently, reducing fuel consumption and emissions. Additionally, these hydrodynamic features enhance stability and manoeuvrability, even in challenging sea conditions.

The propulsion systems of autonomous ships are equally cutting-edge. They incorporate technologies like electric propulsion, pod propulsion, and variable-pitch propellers to fine-tune power delivery and reduce energy waste. These systems are often integrated with advanced control algorithms that adjust propulsion settings in real time based on environmental conditions and operational requirements.

The result of these hydrodynamic innovations is a new era of maritime transportation that is both eco-friendly and economically efficient. Autonomous ships equipped with these designs are pioneers in sustainable shipping, setting the course for a cleaner and more efficient future for the maritime industry.

10. 3D PRINTING

Integrating 3D printing technology into autonomous ships represents a significant leap forward in maintenance and spare parts management. These vessels leverage the power of 3D printing to produce replacement parts on demand, transforming the traditional inventory-heavy approach to maintenance.

Onboard 3D printers can create precise replicas of various ship components, from small nuts and bolts to complex machinery parts. When a part wears out or becomes damaged, crew members can simply input the design specifications into the 3D printer's computer, and within hours, a new, custom-made replacement is ready for installation.

This capability reduces the need for extensive spare parts storage, freeing up valuable onboard space and reducing logistical challenges associated with resupplying remote autonomous vessels. It also enhances maintenance capabilities by significantly reducing downtime. Ships can continue operations while replacement parts are printed, minimising mission disruptions.

Moreover, 3D printing contributes to sustainability by minimising waste. Traditional manufacturing often produces excess materials and packaging, whereas 3D printing generates parts with minimal material waste, promoting a greener approach to maintenance.

Incorporating 3D printing technology into autonomous ships represents a paradigm shift in maintenance practices, improving efficiency, sustainability, and operational flexibility in maritime transportation.

11. ENERGY STORAGE SOLUTIONS

Autonomous ships are at the forefront of energy innovation, incorporating state-of-the-art energy storage solutions that power auxiliary systems and serve as reliable backups in emergencies. These innovative technologies, including advanced batteries and fuel cells, are essential for ensuring uninterrupted operations and enhancing safety at sea.

Advanced batteries, often employing lithium-ion or solid-state technology, are the primary energy source for numerous onboard systems. They provide a clean and efficient power supply for everything from navigation equipment and communication systems to lighting and climate control. These batteries are designed for longevity and reliability, enduring the rigorous demands of maritime environments.

Fuel cells, another key component of the ship's energy storage arsenal, offer a complementary power source. They are especially valuable for extended journeys, as they can generate high energy density electricity from hydrogen or other fuels. In the event of power system failures or emergencies, fuel cells can swiftly assume the role of a backup power supply, ensuring critical functions like navigation, communication, and emergency lighting continue without interruption.

These energy storage solutions represent a dual commitment to efficiency and safety in autonomous shipping. They reduce the vessel's environmental impact by minimising emissions and fuel consumption while bolstering its resilience and readiness for unforeseen challenges on the open sea.

12.   AUGMENTED REALITY (AR)

Augmented Reality (AR) has become an indispensable tool in the world of autonomous ships, transforming maintenance procedures into more efficient, precise, and accessible tasks. AR systems provide crew members and operators with real-time, context-aware data and instructions overlaid with physical equipment, revolutionising maintenance and repairs.

When a maintenance task arises, crew members with AR headsets or devices can access information. AR overlays schematics, diagnostic data, and step-by-step repair instructions directly onto the equipment they are working on. This immersive experience allows technicians to quickly identify issues, follow precise repair procedures, and troubleshoot effectively, reducing downtime and minimising errors.

AR also facilitates remote assistance, where experts onshore or in a central control hub can view the technician's live feed through the AR system. They can provide guidance, mark areas of interest, and even draw virtual annotations to assist in complex repairs, regardless of the ship's location.

The integration of AR into maintenance workflows not only enhances efficiency but also contributes to safety by minimising the risk of human error. It empowers crew members to confidently perform complex tasks, ensuring that autonomous ships remain operational and mission-ready in the most challenging maritime conditions.

13.   OCEANOGRAPHIC INSTRUMENTATION

In the realm of autonomous ships, the incorporation of oceanographic instrumentation represents a vital bridge between maritime technology and scientific exploration. These vessels, often equipped with various specialised instruments, play a pivotal role in advancing our understanding of the world's oceans.

One of the key oceanographic instruments onboard autonomous ships is sonar systems. These sophisticated systems precisely use sound waves to map the ocean floor and the water column. By emitting sound pulses and measuring their return times, sonar technology creates detailed, three-dimensional maps of the seafloor's topography and the distribution of marine life. These maps are invaluable for oceanographers and marine biologists studying the geology, biology, and ecosystems of the ocean.

Deep-sea sensors are another critical component of oceanographic instrumentation. These sensors are designed to withstand the extreme pressures and conditions of the ocean's depths, often reaching depths impossible for humans to explore directly. They measure parameters such as temperature, salinity, pressure, and the presence of specific chemicals. This data is crucial for understanding the complex physical and chemical processes that govern the ocean's behaviour, including ocean circulation, the formation of deep-sea currents, and the effects of climate change on the marine environment.

Autonomous ships equipped with these oceanographic instruments are transportation vessels and advanced research platforms that expand the frontiers of marine science and exploration. They enable scientists to gather data in remote and challenging environments, unveiling the mysteries of the deep sea and contributing to our collective knowledge of the world's oceans. This synergy between technology and scientific inquiry heralds a new era of discovery beneath the waves.

BENEFITS OF AUTONOMOUS SHIPS

Adopting autonomous ships brings forth many advantages, eleven (11) of which stand out prominently.

1. INCREASED SAFETY

Autonomous ships represent a transformative leap in maritime safety. By eliminating the risk of human error, a leading cause of maritime accidents, these vessels significantly enhance safety at sea. Equipped with advanced sensors, radar, lidar, and AI-driven algorithms, autonomous ships can detect and respond to potential hazards in real time. Whether navigating through busy shipping lanes or adverse weather conditions, these vessels can swiftly execute collision avoidance manoeuvres and adjust their courses to ensure safe passage. In emergencies, their rapid response capabilities are unparalleled, mitigating risks and potentially saving lives. As a result, the seas become safer for both autonomous and traditional vessels, reducing the occurrence of accidents and the associated human and environmental costs.

2. ENHANCED EFFICIENCY

Autonomous ships are at the forefront of efficiency optimisation in maritime transportation. Their ability to calculate and adjust routes, speed, and fuel consumption with a precision that surpasses human capabilities leads to several notable benefits. Firstly, they deliver substantial fuel savings, reducing both operational costs and the environmental impact of shipping through reduced greenhouse gas emissions. Secondly, their efficiency extends to overall operational effectiveness. Due to their predictive maintenance capabilities, these vessels are adept at managing cargo loads, optimising schedules, and minimising downtime. Consequently, they offer a level of efficiency and sustainability that is challenging to achieve with conventional manned vessels. By embracing autonomous technology, the maritime industry takes a significant step toward a more environmentally friendly and economically viable future.

3. REDUCED LABOR COSTS

One of the most compelling financial advantages of autonomous ships for shipping companies is the substantial reduction in labour costs. These vessels are designed to operate with smaller or, in some cases, no onboard crews, leading to significant savings. Traditional ships require a crew to navigate, maintain and manage various ship systems, ensuring safety and operational efficiency. In contrast, autonomous ships leverage advanced technologies such as sensors, AI, and remote monitoring, allowing them to perform tasks that would otherwise demand a crew of substantial size.

This cost-effective feature of autonomous ships is particularly advantageous for long-haul and repetitive routes. Shipping companies can allocate resources more efficiently, redirecting funds that would have been spent on salaries, accommodations, and crew welfare toward other critical aspects of their operations. Consequently, they gain a competitive edge by reducing their operational expenses, ultimately benefiting the company's bottom line and, potentially, the pricing of the goods being transported.

4. OPERATIONAL FLEXIBILITY

Another noteworthy benefit of autonomous ships lies in their operational flexibility. These vessels are highly adaptable and capable of swiftly rerouting in response to changing conditions. Autonomous ships can adjust their routes and schedules in real time if faced with adverse weather patterns, congested shipping lanes, or unexpected operational disruptions.

This adaptability minimises delays and ensures the timely delivery of goods, a critical factor in the shipping industry where just-in-time deliveries and tight schedules are the norm. By efficiently circumventing obstacles and optimising their paths, autonomous ships improve supply chain reliability and customer satisfaction.

Furthermore, operational flexibility extends beyond route adjustments. Autonomous ships can also adapt their speed and cargo handling procedures, optimising their operations to meet changing demands and logistical challenges. As a result, shipping companies benefit from enhanced operational resilience, ensuring that goods are delivered on time, every time, even in the face of unpredictable conditions.

5. REMOTE AND HAZARDOUS OPERATIONS

Autonomous ships have emerged as indispensable assets in conducting remote and hazardous operations, notably in domains like offshore oil and gas exploration, where human presence can be perilous. These vessels possess a unique advantage in these challenging environments, as they can navigate and execute tasks with unmatched precision while reducing the inherent risks to human life.

In offshore exploration, for instance, where conditions are often harsh and unpredictable, autonomous ships can deploy specialised equipment and sensors to survey the seabed, monitor environmental conditions, and perform maintenance on underwater infrastructure. These tasks, which would pose significant dangers to human divers and crew members, are executed accurately and without exposing anyone to potential harm.

Furthermore, in hazardous situations such as responding to oil spills, chemical leaks, or other environmental emergencies, autonomous ships can swiftly and effectively carry out containment, monitoring, and cleanup operations without risking human health and safety. This capability transforms the response to such crises, accelerating the mitigation of environmental damage and enhancing overall disaster management.

6. CONTINUOUS OPERATIONS

The inherent nature of autonomous ships allows them to excel in continuous operations. Unlike human crews that require rest, adhere to working hours, and face fatigue limitations, autonomous vessels are designed to operate around the clock. This uninterrupted workflow ensures the consistent and timely transport of goods, minimising delivery times and bolstering the efficiency of maritime transportation.

By eliminating the need for crew shift changes and breaks, autonomous ships can maintain a steady pace throughout their journeys, regardless of duration. This is particularly valuable for long-haul routes spanning vast distances or operations that demand rapid response times. Whether transporting goods across international waters or the timely delivery of critical supplies to remote locations, these vessels offer a level of operational continuity unparalleled in the maritime industry.

The ability to operate continuously reduces transit times and enhances the overall competitiveness of autonomous shipping, making it an attractive option for industries that demand timely and reliable transport services.

7. CARGO SECURITY

Autonomous ships usher in a new era of cargo security, integrating advanced monitoring and security systems that significantly mitigate the risk of theft, damage, or tampering during transit. These vessels are equipped with cutting-edge technology, including a network of sensors, cameras, and secure communication systems, creating a robust framework for safeguarding transported goods.

These advanced cargo monitoring systems provide real-time visibility into the condition and location of the cargo throughout the entire journey. They can detect and report any irregularities, such as unexpected deviations in temperature, humidity, or unexpected shocks. In an anomaly, the autonomous ship's onboard systems can initiate immediate responses, such as alerting security personnel or adjusting environmental controls to mitigate potential damage.

Moreover, these security features extend to preventing unauthorised access to cargo holds. Utilising biometric authentication and secure access controls, autonomous ships ensure that only authorised personnel can access specific areas, adding an extra layer of protection against theft or tampering. The integration of these advanced security measures not only safeguards the interests of shipping companies but also instils confidence in clients, assuring them of the safety and integrity of their transported goods.

8. REDUCED HUMAN FATIGUE

Crew fatigue is a perennial concern in the maritime industry, impacting the safety and efficiency of operations. Autonomous ships address this issue head-on by eliminating the factor of human fatigue. Unlike their human counterparts, autonomous vessels do not experience exhaustion or impaired decision-making due to sleep deprivation.

The continuous operation of autonomous ships, without needing crew shifts and rest periods, ensures that the vessel remains at peak performance levels throughout its journey. Fatigue-related errors, which can lead to accidents or operational inefficiencies, are virtually eliminated, contributing to enhanced safety standards at sea.

This absence of human fatigue also improves decision-making capabilities, particularly in critical situations. Autonomous ships can consistently analyse data, respond to changing conditions, and execute precise manoeuvres without the risk of impaired cognitive functions due to tiredness. This aspect not only elevates the safety of maritime operations but also underscores the considerable benefits of autonomous technology in reducing human-related risks in the shipping industry.

9. ENVIRONMENTAL BENEFITS

Autonomous ships are leading the charge toward a more sustainable future for maritime transportation, offering a range of environmental benefits that align with global efforts to reduce the industry's carbon footprint and promote sustainability.

One of the primary environmental advantages of autonomous ships lies in their ability to optimise routes and fuel consumption with unparalleled precision. Utilising advanced algorithms and real-time data from a network of sensors, these vessels can continuously adjust their course and speed, ensuring the most fuel-efficient journey possible. This reduces greenhouse gas emissions and other pollutants, contributing to cleaner air and a healthier marine ecosystem.

Additionally, autonomous ships often employ alternative propulsion technologies, such as electric or hydrogen fuel cells, which produce minimal or zero emissions during operation. This shift toward cleaner energy sources further reduces maritime transportation's environmental impact, helping combat climate change and reduce the industry's reliance on fossil fuels.

Furthermore, autonomous ships can adopt environmentally friendly practices, such as avoiding sensitive ecological areas or minimising disturbances to marine life. These vessels protect fragile ecosystems and support sustainable marine conservation efforts by adhering to strict navigational guidelines and leveraging their data-driven decision-making capabilities.

10. DATA-DRIVEN INSIGHTS

The data generated by autonomous ships is a valuable resource that goes beyond immediate operational benefits. This wealth of information provides shipping companies with continuous insights into vessel performance, environmental impact, and operational efficiency.

Shipping companies can engage in ongoing performance analysis and improvement by harnessing this data. They can fine-tune their operations, optimise maintenance schedules, and identify areas where fuel efficiency can be enhanced. This data-driven approach reduces costs and ensures vessels operate at their peak potential, minimising their environmental impact.

Moreover, the data collected by autonomous ships can be shared with regulatory authorities and industry organisations, supporting efforts to establish and enforce environmental standards. It facilitates transparency and accountability, allowing stakeholders to track progress toward sustainability goals and make informed decisions to protect the world's oceans and reduce the environmental footprint of maritime transportation.

11. GLOBAL CONNECTIVITY

Autonomous ships have ushered in a new era of global maritime connectivity, empowered by state-of-the-art communication systems that transcend geographical boundaries. These vessels are equipped with an array of advanced technologies that ensure continuous connectivity, even in the most remote and challenging areas of the world's oceans. This unparalleled global connectivity is the linchpin for various critical functions, revolutionising maritime operations.

The advanced communication systems on autonomous ships enable real-time monitoring of vessel status, environmental conditions, and cargo integrity. This means that shipping companies and maritime authorities can maintain constant oversight of their fleets, ensuring that vessels operate efficiently and adhere to safety and environmental regulations. For example, they can monitor fuel consumption, engine performance, and emissions in real time, facilitating proactive adjustments and cost savings.

Navigation assistance is another significant benefit of global connectivity. Autonomous ships can access up-to-date weather forecasts, route information, and navigational data from remote locations, allowing for safer and more efficient journeys. These vessels can receive and analyse data from various sources, including satellites, weather buoys, and coastal monitoring stations, ensuring they make informed decisions to navigate storms, avoid hazards, and optimise their routes.

In the event of emergencies, global connectivity takes on a paramount role. Autonomous ships can transmit distress signals and share vital information with search and rescue teams, coastal authorities, and nearby vessels in real time. This rapid and precise communication enhances the response to emergencies, such as accidents or medical crises, potentially saving lives and reducing the environmental impact of incidents at sea.

In essence, the global connectivity of autonomous ships marks a transformative shift in the maritime industry, enhancing safety, efficiency, and sustainability. By bridging the gap between vessels and the world's interconnected information networks, these ships are leading the way toward a more connected and responsive maritime ecosystem capable of addressing the challenges and opportunities of the modern age.

These benefits collectively demonstrate the transformative potential of autonomous ships in revolutionising maritime transportation, from improved safety and efficiency to environmental sustainability and cost-effectiveness.

CHALLENGES IN THE AUTONOMOUS SHIPPING LANDSCAPE

While promising, the transition to autonomous shipping is accompanied by significant challenges that need to be addressed to ensure the safe and efficient operation of these vessels.

1. LEGAL AND REGULATORY FRAMEWORKS

Perhaps one of the most pressing challenges in the autonomous shipping landscape is the development of comprehensive and internationally recognised legal and regulatory frameworks. These frameworks must govern various aspects of autonomous ship operation, such as safety standards, collision avoidance protocols, and liability in case of accidents. Navigating the complex web of international maritime laws and conventions to accommodate the unique characteristics of autonomous vessels is a formidable task. Ensuring consistency across different jurisdictions and obtaining global acceptance for these frameworks is essential for the widespread adoption of autonomous shipping.

2. CYBERSECURITY CONCERNS

The increasing digital connectivity of autonomous ships brings about a heightened risk of cybersecurity threats. These vessels rely heavily on complex computer systems and networks, which, if compromised, can result in serious consequences, including potential hijacking or sabotage. Protecting against hacking, data breaches, system vulnerabilities, and other cyber threats is paramount. Implementing robust cybersecurity measures, including encryption, intrusion detection systems, and regular security audits, is essential to safeguard these vessels against cyberattacks. As the reliance on digital technology continues to grow, addressing cybersecurity concerns becomes an ongoing challenge that requires continuous vigilance and adaptation.

3. TRUST-BUILDING WITH STAKEHOLDERS

The successful integration of autonomous ships into maritime operations hinges on the crucial factor of trust-building with various stakeholders within the industry. This trust-building process extends to multiple fronts, starting with the ship's crew members. Ensuring that crew members are comfortable with the idea of working alongside or in support of autonomous systems is vital to their successful coexistence. Crew training, communication, and fostering an understanding of how autonomous technology enhances safety and efficiency are essential elements in this endeavour.

Beyond the ship's personnel, trust must be cultivated with regulatory bodies responsible for establishing and enforcing safety standards. Autonomous ships must adhere to comprehensive regulations and guidelines to ensure their safe and responsible operation. Port authorities, too, play a pivotal role in ensuring that autonomous vessels can dock, load, and unload cargo seamlessly and safely. Engaging with these entities to establish industry standards and protocols is essential.

Moreover, gaining the trust of the public is equally paramount. Widespread acceptance of autonomous ships requires transparent communication about the technology's benefits, safety measures, and potential to impact the environment positively. Addressing public concerns about the safety of autonomous vessels and their implications for employment within the maritime industry is critical to fostering support and reducing scepticism.

4. LIABILITY AND INSURANCE CONSIDERATIONS

Navigating the intricate landscape of liability and insurance is another formidable challenge in the realm of autonomous shipping. Determining the appropriate liability structures and insurance mechanisms for autonomous ship accidents or incidents requires significant legal and financial considerations.

Traditional maritime insurance models, which have been honed over decades, may need significant adaptation to accommodate the unique risks posed by autonomous vessels. Questions surrounding liability in technology failures, software glitches, or unforeseen collisions with other vessels must be addressed comprehensively. The responsible party in such scenarios, whether the ship operator, the autonomous technology manufacturer, or a combination thereof, requires careful delineation.

In addition to establishing liability, insurance products must be developed that adequately cover the unique risks associated with autonomous shipping. This involves assessing the likelihood and impact of various incidents and accidents, which may differ from those in traditional maritime operations. Insurers must also consider how technology safeguards and redundancy measures impact risk profiles.

Navigating these challenges in liability and insurance is a critical step in ensuring the sustainable growth and expansion of autonomous shipping. Clear and robust legal and financial frameworks will assure all stakeholders and foster the confidence to embrace this transformative technology in the maritime industry.

5. COMMUNICATION AND COLLABORATION

In the era of autonomous shipping, effective communication and collaboration among various stakeholders in the maritime ecosystem are paramount to ensuring the seamless integration of autonomous vessels into the industry. This collaboration extends to multiple layers of the maritime world, involving shipping companies, technology providers, regulatory bodies, and port authorities.

Shipping companies must work closely with technology providers to adopt and adapt autonomous systems to their specific operational needs. This involves not only the deployment of the technology itself but also understanding how it can be integrated into existing processes and procedures to maximise efficiency and safety. Clear lines of communication between these entities are vital for the successful implementation of autonomous shipping solutions.

Regulatory bodies play a pivotal role in establishing autonomous ships' rules and standards. Close coordination between these bodies and industry players is necessary to ensure the technology aligns with safety and environmental regulations. This collaboration is essential to create a regulatory framework that promotes innovation while upholding stringent safety and environmental standards.

As the gatekeepers of maritime infrastructure, port authorities must also be involved in the conversation. Autonomous vessels must seamlessly interface with port facilities, from docking and cargo handling to security protocols. Coordination between port authorities and shipping companies is essential to facilitate these interactions and ensure the smooth operation of autonomous ships in port environments.

This interconnected collaboration among stakeholders fosters a holistic approach to integrating autonomous vessels, aiming to achieve safety, efficiency, and sustainability in maritime transportation.

6. ETHICAL QUESTIONS

The ascent of autonomous ships inevitably raises ethical questions and concerns that warrant careful consideration. Chief among these ethical dilemmas is the issue of decision-making during emergencies or accidents. Autonomous systems rely on algorithms and AI to make split-second decisions in complex scenarios, raising questions about how these systems prioritise safety, human life, and environmental preservation.

Ensuring the ethical and responsible behaviour of AI and autonomous systems is a pressing concern that requires robust guidelines and ethical frameworks. These frameworks should address questions such as who bears responsibility in cases of AI-driven decisions that result in accidents, how to program systems to prioritise human safety, and what ethical principles should govern AI-driven actions in contexts where human lives are at stake.

Moreover, transparency and accountability in developing and deploying autonomous technology are crucial. Stakeholders must understand how AI systems make decisions and have mechanisms to challenge those decisions when necessary. Ethical considerations also extend to issues like data privacy, cybersecurity, and the potential impact of autonomous shipping on the labour force within the maritime industry.

Addressing these ethical questions as autonomous ships become more prevalent will ensure this transformative technology aligns with our societal values and priorities. Responsible development and deployment of autonomous systems will help us harness the benefits of this technology while upholding our ethical standards and moral obligations.

7. HUMAN ADAPTATION

As the maritime industry undergoes a transformative shift towards autonomous ships, human adaptation emerges as a critical aspect of this transition. Maritime personnel, including ship crew members and operators, are at the heart of this evolution, and their roles are evolving to accommodate this new era of shipping. Ensuring these professionals are adequately trained and equipped to operate and manage autonomous vessels is paramount to the industry's success.

Training and re-skilling programs are fundamental components of this adaptation process. Crew members must learn to collaborate effectively with autonomous systems, understanding their capabilities and limitations. They must also grasp the intricacies of monitoring and supervising these advanced technologies to ensure safe and efficient operations. Furthermore, operators and maintenance personnel require specialised training to handle the sophisticated sensors, AI algorithms, and robotic systems that power these vessels.

Beyond technical training, an emphasis on soft skills is also important. Crew members must develop communication and problem-solving abilities to interact seamlessly with autonomous systems and, when necessary, override them in emergencies. Additionally, adapting to a more data-driven decision-making process will require understanding data analysis and interpretation.

Ultimately, human adaptation to the era of autonomous shipping is a multifaceted endeavour that combines technical proficiency with a mindset shift towards collaboration and adaptability. The successful integration of both human and autonomous capabilities will be key to realising the full potential of this technology.

8. DATA PRIVACY

The widespread adoption of autonomous ships introduces a new frontier of data collection and utilisation in the maritime industry. These vessels are equipped with various sensors and systems that gather vast amounts of data, including cargo information, navigation routes, environmental conditions, and more. While this data is invaluable for operational efficiency and safety, it raises critical concerns regarding data privacy and securing sensitive information.

Protecting data privacy encompasses several key considerations. Firstly, secure data during collection, transmission, and storage to prevent unauthorised access or breaches. Encryption, access controls, and robust cybersecurity measures are essential to safeguarding sensitive information from malicious actors or inadvertent leaks.

Secondly, clear data ownership and consent protocols must be established. It's imperative to define who owns the data generated by autonomous ships and establish mechanisms for obtaining consent when data involves personal or sensitive information. This ensures that data usage complies with legal and ethical standards.

Furthermore, the industry must address the potential misuse of data by defining strict guidelines for data sharing and resale. Data generated by autonomous ships can have far-reaching implications, from optimising supply chains to impacting environmental policies. Careful consideration of how data is shared, with whom, and under what conditions is crucial to prevent data exploitation or unintended consequences.

In the era of autonomous shipping, data privacy is not just a technical issue but a complex ethical, legal, and social concern. Striking the right balance between harnessing the power of data for innovation and protecting individuals' privacy rights will be a defining challenge for the industry.

9. ENVIRONMENTAL IMPACT

The adoption of autonomous ships represents a pivotal step in enhancing the environmental sustainability of the maritime industry. These vessels offer substantial benefits through route optimisation, fuel efficiency, and reduced greenhouse gas emissions during operational lifetimes. However, there is a critical consideration regarding the environmental impact associated with the manufacturing and disposal of the advanced technologies and batteries used in these autonomous vessels.

Manufacturing and sourcing the components and materials needed for autonomous technology, such as sensors, AI systems, and lithium-ion batteries, can entail resource-intensive processes. These processes may involve the extraction of rare minerals and metals, which can have ecological consequences, including habitat disruption and pollution. Additionally, the energy-intensive production of batteries raises concerns about carbon emissions during the manufacturing phase.

Disposing of outdated or damaged technology from autonomous ships also raises environmental concerns. Proper disposal methods and recycling mechanisms are vital to minimise electronic waste and prevent hazardous materials from entering landfills or contaminating ecosystems. Therefore, the maritime industry must adopt sustainable practices in designing, manufacturing, and disposing of autonomous ship technology to ensure that adverse impacts during the product life cycle do not offset the environmental benefits realised during operation.

10. TECHNOLOGICAL HURDLES

The successful integration of autonomous ships into the maritime industry hinges on overcoming a series of formidable technological hurdles. Ensuring the reliability of AI algorithms, sensors' robustness, and autonomous systems' resilience to extreme maritime conditions is paramount to guarantee their safe and effective operation.

AI algorithms, the backbone of autonomous decision-making, must be rigorously tested and refined to handle various complex scenarios, including adverse weather conditions, heavy maritime traffic, and unexpected emergencies. Ensuring these algorithms can adapt to dynamic environments and unforeseen circumstances is essential for operational safety.

Furthermore, the sensors and sensor fusion technologies that provide critical data inputs to autonomous systems must be capable of withstanding the harsh and unpredictable conditions of the open sea. Saltwater corrosion, extreme temperatures, and seawater's corrosive effects can challenge these sensors' durability.

Resilience to system failures is another vital aspect. Autonomous ships must be equipped with redundancy measures and fail-safe mechanisms to prevent catastrophic incidents in the event of sensor malfunctions or software glitches.

Overcoming these technological challenges is an ongoing and collaborative effort involving maritime technology providers, research institutions, and regulatory bodies. By addressing these hurdles, the maritime industry can ensure that autonomous ships enhance efficiency and safety and meet the stringent requirements for reliable and robust operations at sea.

CHAPTER 3

AUTONOMOUS SHIP MANAGEMENT COMPANIES

The maritime industry is undergoing a profound transformation with the advent of autonomous ships, heralding a new era in maritime transportation. As these technologically advanced vessels become a reality, the role of ship management has evolved significantly to accommodate the unique challenges and opportunities of autonomous shipping. Within this evolving landscape, Autonomous Ship Management Companies have emerged as pivotal players, offering a comprehensive suite of services integral to the safe, efficient, and responsible operation of these cutting-edge vessels.

These Autonomous Ship Management Companies are crucial in ensuring that autonomous ships navigate the seas seamlessly while adhering to stringent safety and regulatory standards. Their services encompass various responsibilities, including monitoring onboard systems, real-time data analysis, predictive maintenance, route optimisation, and cybersecurity. They oversee the intricate dance of sensors, AI algorithms, and robotic systems that drive these vessels, ensuring that everything functions harmoniously.

In this chapter, we delve into the multifaceted services provided by Autonomous Ship Management Companies, shedding light on their pivotal role in shaping the future of maritime transportation. We explore the industry's key players, highlighting the expertise and innovations propelling this sector forward. Moreover, we delve into the collaborative efforts forging partnerships between technology providers, shipping companies, regulatory bodies, and research institutions. These collaborations are instrumental in establishing the best practices, safety standards, and regulatory frameworks to govern the autonomous shipping industry, ensuring its sustainable growth and long-term success.

As autonomous ships continue to evolve and proliferate, the ship management landscape will remain dynamic and responsive to the ever-changing demands of this technology-driven era. This chapter comprehensively explores the services, players, and collaborative endeavours that define autonomous ship management's current and future state, offering insights into how this transformative industry is charting a new course for maritime transportation.

SERVICES PROVIDED BY AUTONOMOUS SHIP MANAGEMENT COMPANIES

REMOTE MONITORING AND CONTROL CENTRES

At the heart of Autonomous Ship Management Companies' services are state-of-the-art remote monitoring and control centres. These centres serve as nerve centres for autonomous vessels, providing 24/7 surveillance and supervision. Highly trained personnel in these control centres act as the eyes and ears of the vessels, continuously tracking their movements and vital parameters. They collect real-time data from many onboard sensors, including navigation, propulsion, weather conditions, and cargo status.

The critical role of these control centres extends to intervention when necessary. In cases where an anomaly or emergency arises, the remote monitoring teams can swiftly and remotely take control of the vessel's systems to ensure safe navigation and mitigate risks. This intervention capability is crucial in scenarios ranging from collision avoidance in congested waters to responding to equipment malfunctions or unexpected environmental challenges. The combination of continuous vigilance and the ability to take decisive action underscores the commitment of Autonomous Ship Management Companies to the safety and efficiency of autonomous maritime operations.

REMOTE DIAGNOSTICS AND MAINTENANCE

Autonomous Ship Management Companies leverage advanced diagnostic tools and remote access capabilities to offer an invaluable real-time remote diagnostics and maintenance service. In essence, they serve as virtual technicians capable of identifying and diagnosing technical issues as they occur onboard autonomous vessels. These companies can access the ship's systems through a secure connection and gather diagnostic data from sensors, machinery, and software components.

The ability to initiate troubleshooting procedures from onshore locations is a game-changer in minimising downtime and operational disruptions. When an issue is detected, the remote teams can swiftly pinpoint the root cause, whether it's a sensor malfunction, software glitch, or mechanical fault. Depending on the situation, they can remotely implement solutions, ranging from recalibrating sensors to conducting software updates or repairs. This rapid response ensures that autonomous vessels remain mission-ready, even in the face of unexpected challenges.

SYSTEM INTEGRATION AND OPTIMIZATION

Autonomous Ship Management Companies play a pivotal role in ensuring the harmonious interplay of the myriad systems aboard autonomous vessels. System integration and optimisation are at the core of their services, and they are dedicated to ensuring that every component, from navigation and communication to propulsion and safety systems, operates seamlessly and synergistically.

Achieving this level of integration is no small feat, as autonomous ships rely on a complex ecosystem of sensors, AI algorithms, and software-driven components. These companies undertake the meticulous task of configuring and fine-tuning these systems to achieve optimal performance and safety. They ensure that communication systems can transmit and receive critical data reliably, that propulsion systems respond precisely to navigational commands, and that safety protocols are seamlessly integrated to respond to emergencies effectively.

In essence, Autonomous Ship Management Companies act as orchestrators of technology, ensuring that the sum of the parts results in a cohesive and efficient vessel. This integration and optimisation process is fundamental to realising the full potential of autonomous ships, enhancing their safety, reliability, and overall effectiveness in maritime transportation.

DATA ANALYTICS FOR PERFORMANCE ANALYSIS

The data generated during the operation of autonomous ships is a valuable resource, and Autonomous Ship Management Companies are at the forefront of harnessing its potential. Leveraging sophisticated data analytics tools and techniques, these companies offer a service beyond mere data collection.

They delve deep into the data, mining it for insights to drive informed decision-making and operational excellence.

One of the primary areas where data analytics shines is performance analysis. Autonomous ships generate vast amounts of data on their operations, including navigation routes, weather conditions, cargo status, and system performance. Autonomous Ship Management Companies use advanced analytics to process and analyse this data comprehensively.

They provide insights into route optimisation, allowing for more fuel-efficient journeys and reduced environmental impact. Additionally, they assist in proactive maintenance planning by identifying potential issues before they become critical and minimising downtime and operational disruptions.

The application of data analytics extends to enhancing overall operational efficiency. By identifying trends, patterns, and opportunities for improvement within the data, these companies empower shipping companies to make data-driven decisions that optimise their operations. This service is invaluable in a rapidly evolving maritime landscape, providing the means to adapt and thrive in an era where data is a strategic asset for success.

CREW TRAINING FOR TRANSITION AND USING NEW TECHNOLOGY IN TRAINING

In acknowledgement of the pivotal role human expertise plays in the transition to autonomous shipping, Autonomous Ship Management Companies have developed specialised crew training programs. These programs bridge the traditional maritime world and the cutting-edge technology that defines autonomous vessels. They assist maritime personnel in adapting to new technologies and equip them with the knowledge and skills to operate and manage autonomous ships effectively.

The training provided by these companies encompasses a broad spectrum of topics. Crew members are educated on the intricacies of autonomous systems, including sensors, AI algorithms, and robotic technologies. They learn to interface with and supervise these advanced systems, ensuring they can effectively collaborate with technology for safe and efficient operations. Additionally, training programs emphasise the importance of decision-making in scenarios where human intervention may be necessary, further enhancing crew members' capabilities in managing autonomous vessels.

Moreover, these companies employ new technologies themselves to enhance crew training. Virtual reality (VR) and augmented reality (AR) simulations enable maritime personnel to immerse themselves in realistic scenarios, providing hands-on experience in a risk-free environment. These training tools offer a dynamic and interactive way to familiarise crew members with the technology they will encounter onboard autonomous ships, enhancing their confidence and competence in managing these vessels.

USING AI AND NEW TECHNOLOGIES TO IMPROVE MANAGEMENT AND OPERATION OF THE VESSELS

Autonomous Ship Management Companies are at the forefront of leveraging artificial intelligence (AI) and emerging technologies to enhance autonomous vessels' management and operation continually. These advanced technologies are harnessed to optimise various vessel operations, contributing to heightened safety and efficiency.

AI-driven algorithms play a central role in this endeavour. These algorithms enable predictive maintenance, which involves analysing real-time data from sensors to anticipate equipment failures or maintenance needs before they occur. This proactive approach minimises downtime, reduces maintenance costs, and ensures critical systems remain in peak condition, enhancing operational reliability.

Advanced route planning is another area where AI shines. Autonomous Ship Management Companies utilise AI to analyse vast datasets, including weather conditions, sea currents, and vessel performance metrics, to chart optimal routes. These routes are fuel-efficient and consider safety and environmental factors, contributing to reduced greenhouse gas emissions and minimising environmental impact.

Real-time decision-making is yet another facet of AI application. AI algorithms constantly process data from onboard sensors and external sources, enabling autonomous vessels to make informed decisions in rapidly changing conditions. This real-time responsiveness ensures safe navigation, collision avoidance, and efficient cargo handling, all while adapting to dynamic maritime environments.

By harnessing AI and emerging technologies, Autonomous Ship Management Companies elevate vessel management and operation to new levels of sophistication and effectiveness. This synergy of human expertise and advanced technology empowers the maritime industry to navigate the seas with unprecedented safety, efficiency, and sustainability.

SAFETY AND EMERGENCY PROTOCOLS

Safety is the foremost priority in autonomous shipping, and Autonomous Ship Management Companies are dedicated to upholding this paramount principle. These companies establish and rigorously enforce a comprehensive suite of safety protocols and fail-safe mechanisms to ensure the utmost protection of autonomous vessels, their cargo, and the marine environment.

Safety protocols encompass many measures, including collision avoidance systems, navigation redundancy, and emergency response procedures. Autonomous ships have sensors and AI algorithms that continuously monitor their surroundings. In the event of unforeseen circumstances or potential collisions, these systems are programmed to take immediate corrective action, such as altering course or adjusting speed to avoid accidents.

Furthermore, Autonomous Ship Management Companies work to ensure that their vessels are prepared to respond effectively to emergencies. This includes mechanisms for fire suppression, man-overboard situations, and even environmental crises such as oil spills. The integration of robotics and remote access capabilities allows for swift and precise responses, minimising the impact of emergencies on both the vessel and the marine ecosystem.

The commitment to safety extends beyond the technological aspects. Crew members are trained to intervene in emergencies, with protocols to facilitate decision-making and actions. These companies conduct regular drills and simulations to ensure crew members are well-prepared to handle various contingencies, from machinery failures to extreme weather events. In essence, Autonomous Ship Management Companies leave no stone unturned in their quest to establish a safety culture that permeates every aspect of autonomous shipping.

REGULATORY COMPLIANCE

Navigating the complex landscape of maritime regulations is a formidable challenge, and Autonomous Ship Management Companies take on this task with diligence and expertise. These companies work tirelessly to ensure that autonomous vessels adhere to many safety, security, environmental, and navigation standards that govern the maritime industry.

Collaboration is key in this endeavour, as these companies forge close partnerships with regulatory authorities, classification societies, and international maritime organisations. They actively engage in dialogue with these entities to facilitate the seamless integration of autonomous vessels into existing regulatory frameworks. This collaborative approach extends to developing new regulations specifically tailored to autonomous shipping, ensuring that safety standards and operational protocols align with the unique challenges and capabilities of autonomous ships.

Ensuring regulatory compliance involves a comprehensive understanding of global and regional maritime laws. These companies stay up-to-date with evolving regulations, keeping abreast of changes in safety and environmental standards, cybersecurity requirements, and navigation protocols. They also contribute their expertise to the regulatory process by providing insights, data, and best practices that inform the development of regulations that foster innovation while safeguarding maritime safety and the environment.

By meticulously adhering to regulatory compliance, Autonomous Ship Management Companies exemplify their commitment to responsible and sustainable autonomous shipping. Their collaborative efforts contribute to creating a regulatory framework that balances safety, innovation, and environmental stewardship, ensuring the continued growth and success of autonomous vessels in the maritime industry.

CONTINUOUS INNOVATION

At the heart of Autonomous Ship Management Companies' ethos lies a commitment to continuous innovation. These companies recognise that technology evolves rapidly and are determined to stay at the forefront of this ever-changing landscape. They invest significantly in research and development, dedicating resources to creating and implementing new technologies that push the boundaries of what autonomous ships can achieve.

Innovation is woven into the fabric of these companies' operations. They constantly explore emerging technologies, from AI and machine learning to advanced sensors and communication systems, to identify how they can be harnessed to enhance the capabilities and safety of autonomous vessels. This forward-looking approach ensures that their fleets remain cutting-edge and competitive in a dynamic industry.

Research and development efforts encompass various facets of autonomous shipping. Autonomous Ship Management Companies explore novel ways to improve navigation and collision avoidance, optimise fuel efficiency, enhance cargo handling, and reduce environmental impact. They are at the vanguard of developing and integrating robotics for tasks such as cargo handling, inspections, and maintenance, augmenting the operational capabilities of their vessels.

Moreover, innovation extends to cybersecurity and data management. With the increasing reliance on data for decision-making and vessel operations, these companies invest in robust cybersecurity measures to protect against potential threats. They also refine data analytics capabilities to extract deeper insights from the vast data generated during ship operations, contributing to more informed decision-making and continuous improvement.

In essence, the commitment to continuous innovation ensures that Autonomous Ship Management Companies remain agile and adaptive in an industry undergoing rapid transformation. It positions them as leaders in integrating cutting-edge technology into maritime operations, ultimately enhancing the safety, efficiency, and sustainability of autonomous shipping.

KEY PLAYERS IN THE INDUSTRY

1. TECHNOLOGY COMPANIES (E.G., ROLLS-ROYCE, KONGSBERG)

Prominent technology companies, such as Rolls-Royce and Kongsberg, play a pivotal role in shaping the landscape of autonomous ship management. These industry giants are at the forefront of developing the advanced technologies that underpin autonomous shipping. They bring extensive expertise in designing and manufacturing autonomous navigation systems, high-precision sensors, AI-driven software, and robotic solutions.

Collaboration between technology companies and ship management firms is instrumental in advancing autonomous ship capabilities. Technology companies provide cutting-edge solutions that enable autonomous vessels to navigate, communicate, and make decisions autonomously. They work closely with ship management companies to integrate these technologies seamlessly into the vessels' operations, ensuring they meet the highest safety and performance standards.

Rolls-Royce and Kongsberg, among others, are renowned for their innovation and commitment to pushing the boundaries of maritime technology. Their contributions to the autonomous ship management industry extend beyond hardware and software; they also actively participate in collaborative efforts to establish industry standards and regulatory frameworks that promote the safe and responsible adoption of autonomous shipping.

2. MARITIME SERVICE PROVIDERS

Established maritime service providers have expanded their offerings to include autonomous ship management services. Leveraging their extensive experience in vessel management, maintenance, logistics, and supply chain operations, these companies have diversified to support the growing fleet of autonomous vessels.

Maritime service providers bring industry-specific knowledge and capabilities to the autonomous ship management sector. They understand the intricacies of vessel operations, crew management, and compliance with maritime regulations. This expertise positions them as valuable partners in the transition to autonomous shipping, as they can seamlessly integrate autonomous vessels into existing maritime ecosystems.

These companies offer various services, including remote monitoring and control, crew training, maintenance, and route optimisation. Their role is to ensure the safe, efficient, and reliable operation of autonomous vessels while optimising operational costs and minimising risks. By bridging the gap between traditional maritime operations and the era of autonomy, maritime service providers are instrumental in facilitating the smooth integration of autonomous ships into the industry.

3.   SHIPPING COMPANIES' INVOLVEMENT

Shipping companies are increasingly active in the autonomous ship management sector, recognising the substantial benefits and opportunities that autonomous vessels bring to their fleets. These shipping companies are driven by several compelling factors that motivate their engagement in autonomous ship management.

- Cost Savings. Autonomous ships offer the potential for significant cost savings in the long term. Reduced labour costs, increased operational efficiency, and optimised fuel consumption can translate into improved profitability for shipping companies.

- Improved Safety. Autonomous vessels are equipped with advanced sensors and AI systems that enhance safety by reducing the risk of human error. Shipping companies are drawn to the prospect of safer maritime operations and a reduced likelihood of accidents at sea.

- Operational Efficiency. Autonomous ships can optimise routes, respond to changing weather conditions, and quickly adapt to traffic congestion. This efficiency minimises delays, ensures timely delivery of goods, and enhances the overall efficiency of shipping operations.

- Environmental Benefits. The fuel efficiency and optimised routing capabilities of autonomous vessels can reduce greenhouse gas emissions. This aligns with shipping companies' goals of improving environmental sustainability and meeting stringent emissions regulations.

Shipping companies are actively exploring partnerships with technology providers and autonomous ship management firms to integrate autonomous vessels into their fleets. These collaborations involve adapting their operational processes, training their crews to work alongside autonomous systems, and ensuring compliance with maritime regulations.

4.   RESEARCH AND DEVELOPMENT COLLABORATIONS

Collaborative efforts between industry leaders, research institutions, and government agencies drive innovation in autonomous ship management. These partnerships catalyse technological advancements, safety protocols, and standardised approaches within the autonomous shipping landscape.

- Technology Advancements. Research collaborations foster the development of cutting-edge technologies, including more reliable sensors, advanced AI algorithms, and enhanced communication systems. These innovations are crucial for ensuring the robustness and effectiveness of autonomous vessels.

31

- Safety Protocols. Safety remains a paramount concern in autonomous shipping. Collaborative research contributes to developing comprehensive safety protocols and fail-safe mechanisms that address the unique challenges posed by autonomous vessels.

- Standardised Approaches. Standardisation is essential for the widespread acceptance and integration of autonomous ships. Collaborations between industry stakeholders and regulatory bodies help establish standardised approaches to autonomous ship management, ensuring consistency and compliance with international maritime regulations.

- Regulatory Frameworks. Collaborative endeavours between industry leaders and regulatory authorities result in the development of regulatory frameworks specifically tailored to autonomous shipping. These frameworks address safety, cybersecurity, crew training, and environmental standards, providing a clear path for adopting autonomous vessels.

Research and development collaborations are fundamental to the responsible and sustainable growth of the autonomous ship management industry. They contribute to creating a safe and supportive ecosystem that enables the seamless integration of autonomous vessels into maritime operations while upholding the highest safety and environmental stewardship standards.

In the rapidly evolving world of autonomous shipping, these companies and their services are pivotal to the success and safety of autonomous vessels. Their expertise, commitment to innovation and collaboration with industry stakeholders steer the maritime industry toward a future where autonomous ships are integral to global trade and transportation.

Chapter 4

IMPACT ON MARITIME INDUSTRY

he maritime industry, steeped in tradition and history, is undergoing a profound transformation—driven by technology's relentless march. At the forefront of this transformation are autonomous ships, vessels that have shattered conventional paradigms and are rewriting the narrative of maritime transportation. In this chapter, we embark on a journey to understand the seismic impact that autonomous ships unleash upon the maritime sector. This impact reverberates through various dimensions, from the accelerated adoption of autonomous vessels to evolving maritime jobs and skillsets.

We delve into the environmental benefits, where sustainability meets innovation and the economic implications that ripple across the industry. As we navigate these uncharted waters, we uncover a landscape forever altered by the autonomous wave. This landscape demands a fresh perspective and an unwavering commitment to embrace the future of maritime transportation.

Join us as we explore how the maritime industry is being reshaped by technology, vision, ambition, and a quest for a more efficient, sustainable, and economically vibrant future.

INCREASED ADOPTION OF AUTONOMOUS SHIPS

The maritime industry is in the midst of a sweeping transformation, and at its heart lies the increasing adoption of autonomous ships. This paradigm shift, driven by technological advancements and a growing recognition of the benefits, reshapes how goods are transported across the world's oceans. Let's delve into the factors propelling this surge in adoption.

1. SAFETY ENHANCEMENT

The primary catalyst driving the increasing adoption of autonomous ships is the substantial promise of heightened safety at sea. These cutting-edge vessels represent a paradigm shift in maritime safety thanks to their integration of advanced sensors, artificial intelligence, and precision navigation systems. One of the most compelling aspects of autonomous ships is their remarkable ability to mitigate the risk of human error, a pervasive contributor to maritime accidents. With the capacity to navigate autonomously, these vessels excel in avoiding collisions, adapting to dynamic conditions, and responding rapidly to emergencies. By seamlessly integrating data from an array of sensors, they maintain unparalleled vigilance over their surroundings, identifying potential hazards and proactively taking evasive actions when necessary. As a result, autonomous ships are fundamentally altering the safety landscape of the maritime industry, ushering in an era characterised by a remarkable reduction in accidents and a significant enhancement of maritime safety standards.

2. OPERATIONAL EFFICIENCY

The term "operational efficiency" finds its perfect embodiment in autonomous ships. These vessels epitomise the marriage of technology and efficiency, offering a multifaceted approach to optimising maritime operations. At their core, autonomous ships are driven by intricate algorithms that tirelessly work to streamline every facet of their journeys. They meticulously calculate and adjust routes to circumvent obstacles, manage speed and propulsion systems with unprecedented precision, and even fine-tune cargo distribution to ensure optimal stability. This meticulous orchestration translates into a cascade of operational benefits that ripple through the maritime industry. Perhaps the most immediately tangible outcome is the remarkable fuel savings that autonomous ships achieve. Their capacity to chart the most fuel-efficient courses, adapt to changing weather conditions, and optimise engine performance leads to substantial reductions in fuel consumption. Beyond cost savings, these optimised routes also reduce voyage durations, making transporting goods more swiftly and reliably possible. In essence, autonomous ships usher in a new era of operational efficiency that benefits shipping companies' bottom lines and contributes to a more sustainable and responsive maritime transportation ecosystem.

3. COST SAVINGS

The allure of cost savings is a magnetic force propelling shipping companies toward adopting autonomous vessels. One of the most striking aspects of these autonomous marvels is their potential to deliver substantial financial benefits. A primary contributor to these savings is the reduced or, in some cases, entirely automated crew requirements. By minimising the need for onboard personnel, labour costs are substantially curtailed, freeing up resources that can be channelled elsewhere in the shipping operation. This labour cost reduction represents a considerable financial advantage and positions autonomous shipping as a cost-effective solution for long-haul and repetitive routes, where crew expenses traditionally loom large.

Another pivotal source of cost savings stems from implementing predictive maintenance and real-time diagnostics. Autonomous ships are equipped with advanced sensors and diagnostic tools that continuously monitor the health of onboard systems. In the event of potential issues or anomalies, these systems trigger alerts, enabling timely intervention and maintenance. Consequently, downtime is minimised, and maintenance expenses are significantly lowered. The cumulative effect of reduced labour costs and optimised maintenance translates into a financially appealing proposition for shipping companies, bolstering the economic case for embracing autonomous vessels as a strategic component of their fleets.

4. TECHNOLOGICAL MATURATION

The maturation of autonomous ship technologies is a transformative force reshaping the maritime landscape. This evolution is marked by a journey from nascent concepts to reliable, accessible, and trusted solutions. Shipping companies are increasingly recognising the significance of this technological maturation, and their growing confidence in the capabilities of autonomous vessels is driving increased investments and widespread adoption.

Leading technology providers like Rolls-Royce and Kongsberg are pivotal players in advancing the technological frontier of autonomous shipping. Their relentless pursuit of innovation and extensive research and development initiatives propel the sector forward. These companies are pushing the boundaries of what is technically achievable and refining the reliability and robustness of autonomous systems.

As a result, shipping companies are gaining the confidence to embrace autonomous vessels as a viable and advantageous addition to their fleets. The maturation of autonomous ship technologies ensures that these vessels are not mere novelties but robust, dependable tools that meet and exceed industry standards. This increased accessibility and reliability pave the way for broader adoption, heralding a future where autonomous shipping is an integral and indispensable part of the maritime industry.

5. REGULATORY ADAPTATION

The journey towards widespread adoption of autonomous ships is intrinsically tied to regulatory adaptation. Regulatory authorities worldwide are keenly aware of the transformative potential of autonomous vessels and are working diligently to adapt existing maritime regulations to accommodate these cutting-edge technologies. This regulatory evolution is a dynamic process that involves international and regional collaboration to provide greater clarity and guidance to the maritime industry.

One of the primary outcomes of this regulatory adaptation is the assurance it offers to shipping companies. As regulatory frameworks evolve and mature, they address critical aspects of autonomous shipping, including safety standards, cybersecurity protocols, crew training requirements, and environmental considerations. This evolving regulatory landscape provides shipping companies with a clear roadmap, assuring them of the legality and safety of adopting autonomous vessels.

Furthermore, regulatory adaptation fosters an environment of trust and accountability. It instils confidence in shipping companies that autonomous vessels will operate within well-defined boundaries and adhere to internationally recognised safety and environmental standards. This trust in the regulatory process is pivotal in encouraging shipping companies to embrace autonomy as a strategic and viable option for their fleets.

6. PROVEN SUCCESS STORIES

A growing collection of proven success stories in various maritime sectors further fuels the allure of autonomous shipping. These real-world implementations of autonomous vessels, spanning container shipping, offshore operations, and research vessels, serve as compelling and tangible evidence of the transformative potential of autonomy.

Each successful implementation represents a milestone in the journey toward autonomous shipping. These vessels have demonstrated their ability to navigate safely and efficiently, even in challenging conditions. Container ships have optimised cargo handling, offshore operations have achieved precision and efficiency, and research vessels have collected valuable data for scientific exploration.

These real-world success stories are more than just case studies; they are beacons of inspiration and confidence for the maritime industry. Shipping companies witness the tangible benefits of autonomy, including enhanced safety, operational efficiency, and cost savings. As a result, they are encouraged to explore the opportunities and advantages that autonomous vessels can bring to their specific operations. The proven successes serve as a testament to the feasibility and potential of autonomous shipping, accelerating its acceptance and integration into the maritime ecosystem.

7. ENVIRONMENTAL CONSIDERATIONS

The maritime industry faces mounting pressure to address its environmental impact, and autonomous ships emerge as a compelling solution to meet these sustainability challenges head-on. These vessels, equipped with advanced technologies such as route optimisation and fuel efficiency management, align perfectly with the industry's drive to reduce its environmental footprint.

Shipping companies are increasingly recognising the multifaceted environmental benefits of autonomous ships. Their advanced algorithms meticulously calculate the most fuel-efficient routes, accounting for weather conditions and sea currents. This optimisation minimises fuel consumption and, consequently, reduces greenhouse gas emissions. As such, autonomous vessels represent a significant step towards achieving sustainability goals and contributing to a more environmentally friendly future for the maritime industry.

Moreover, the environmental considerations extend beyond emissions reduction. Through their precision and ability to respond to changing conditions in real time, autonomous ships are better equipped to prevent environmental accidents, such as oil spills or collisions with marine wildlife. This proactive approach to environmental stewardship further solidifies the role of autonomous vessels as a responsible and sustainable choice for shipping companies.

8. COMPETITIVE ADVANTAGE

Maintaining a competitive edge in the fiercely competitive global shipping market is a formidable driving force behind adopting autonomous technology. Early adopters of autonomous ships gain a strategic advantage by positioning themselves at the vanguard of industry innovation.

This competitive advantage stems from several key factors. First and foremost is the enhancement of operational efficiency. With their meticulous route optimisation, reduced downtime, and streamlined cargo handling, autonomous ships offer a level of efficiency that sets them apart. This translates into cost savings and improved reliability, compelling attributes that resonate with shipping companies and their clients.

Furthermore, early adopters demonstrate a commitment to innovation and a forward-thinking approach, which can be leveraged as a market differentiator. They become industry trailblazers, showcasing their readiness to embrace technology-driven solutions that provide tangible benefits. This positioning can attract new clients and enhance relationships with existing ones, solidifying their status as leaders in the maritime sector.

The quest for a competitive advantage is a powerful motivator for shipping companies to adopt autonomous technology. Those who embrace these cutting-edge solutions stand to gain operational efficiencies, cost savings, and a strategic foothold in an evolving and increasingly dynamic global shipping landscape.

The increased adoption of autonomous ships is a testament to their potential to revolutionise maritime transportation. As more shipping companies embark on the journey towards autonomy, the maritime industry stands on the cusp of a transformative era where safety, efficiency, and innovation define its evolution.

EVOLUTION OF MARITIME JOBS AND SKILLSETS

Integrating autonomous ships into the maritime industry is ushering in a profound transformation in how vessels are operated and the roles and skillsets required within the maritime workforce. This evolution reflects the industry's adaptation to the changing technological landscape and the imperative to remain competitive and innovative. Let's explore how maritime jobs and the skills needed are undergoing a fundamental shift.

1. EMERGENCE OF AUTONOMOUS VESSEL OPERATORS

The maritime industry is undergoing a remarkable transformation with the emergence of a new breed of professionals known as autonomous vessel operators. These individuals are pivotal in the brave new world of autonomous shipping, where technology and maritime expertise converge. Their responsibilities are diverse and multifaceted, reflecting the intricate nature of overseeing autonomous systems and ensuring the seamless operation of these cutting-edge vessels.

Autonomous vessel operators are tasked with the critical mission of monitoring vessel operations from remote control centres. From these digital command hubs, they serve as the vigilant overseers of autonomous systems, constantly keeping a watchful eye on vessel movements and performance. Their role extends beyond mere observation; they possess the authority and capability to intervene swiftly and effectively. This intervention may encompass a range of actions, from adjusting navigation parameters to responding to unforeseen circumstances or emergencies.

Their unique fusion of maritime expertise and technological proficiency sets these professionals apart. They bridge the gap between the maritime traditions of navigation, safety, and seamanship and the cutting-edge world of artificial intelligence, sensors, and automation. This dynamic blend of skills ensures that autonomous vessels are not just autonomous but also meticulously supervised, adding an extra layer of safety and reliability to their operations. As autonomous shipping continues to advance, the role of autonomous vessel operators is poised to become increasingly prominent, underlining the industry's commitment to responsible autonomy.

2. DATA ANALYSTS AND REMOTE MONITORING SPECIALISTS

The advent of autonomous ships has ushered in an era of data abundance, and at the heart of this data-rich environment stand data analysts and remote monitoring specialists. These professionals are pivotal in navigating the sea of information generated during autonomous ship voyages, transforming raw data into actionable insights that optimise vessel performance and ensure safety.

Data analysts are the architects of knowledge within the realm of autonomous shipping. They harness their analytical prowess to make sense of the vast amounts of data streaming in from onboard sensors, communication systems, and navigation equipment. Through meticulous analysis, they identify trends, anomalies, and performance indicators that guide decision-making. These insights are instrumental in optimising routes, fuel efficiency, and maintenance planning, ultimately contributing to enhanced operational efficiency and cost savings.

Remote monitoring specialists are the guardians of autonomous vessel operations. Their vigilant oversight ensures that vessel systems are functioning seamlessly. They detect irregularities or deviations from expected behaviour in real time and initiate responses as needed. These specialists work closely with autonomous vessel operators and technology providers to maintain the highest levels of safety and reliability during voyages.

In essence, data analysts and remote monitoring specialists are the unsung heroes of autonomous shipping, working diligently behind the scenes to ensure the success and safety of these advanced vessels. Their expertise in data analysis and real-time monitoring is indispensable in harnessing the full potential of autonomous ships while upholding the industry's commitment to maritime safety and operational excellence.

3. TECHNICIANS SPECIALIZING IN ONBOARD TECHNOLOGY

As the evolution of autonomous ships accelerates, a new breed of maritime professionals is rising to prominence. technicians specialising in onboard technology. These highly skilled technicians are responsible for maintaining, repairing, and troubleshooting the intricate web of advanced technology that powers autonomous vessels.

At the heart of their role lies the meticulous care and maintenance of the onboard technology infrastructure. Autonomous ships have diverse cutting-edge systems, including high-precision sensors, AI-driven decision-making systems, and state-of-the-art communication equipment. These technicians must ensure that these systems function at peak performance. Their daily tasks include regular inspections, preventive maintenance routines, and swift responses to technical issues.

In a malfunction or technical hiccup, technicians specialising in onboard technology are the first responders. Their expertise is tested as they diagnose the problem, execute repairs, and swiftly implement fixes to restore full functionality. Their ability to troubleshoot and resolve issues is about keeping the vessel operational and upholding safety standards, as many of these systems are integral to collision avoidance, navigation, and emergency responses.

As autonomous ships continue to advance in complexity and sophistication, the role of technicians specialising in onboard technology becomes paramount. They are the unsung heroes ensuring the reliability and resilience of these vessels, underpinning the industry's commitment to safe and efficient autonomy.

4. TRAINING AND TRANSITION SPECIALISTS

The maritime industry is at the cusp of a significant transformation, transitioning from traditional seafaring to the era of autonomous shipping. In this transformative landscape, training and transition specialists take centre stage. These dedicated professionals are pivotal in preparing maritime personnel to operate and manage autonomous vessels effectively, facilitating a seamless transition into this new era.

The responsibilities of training and transition specialists are multifaceted and encompass a wide range of activities. They design and implement specialised training programs that equip mariners with the knowledge and skills to work alongside autonomous systems. These programs cover various aspects, including understanding the technology onboard, utilising AI-driven navigation tools, and mastering emergency response procedures in the context of autonomy.

One of their key objectives is to bridge the gap between traditional maritime practices and the emerging technologies that define autonomous shipping. They facilitate the cultural shift within maritime organisations, ensuring that mariners embrace and adapt to the changes brought about by autonomy. This includes instilling a deep understanding of safety protocols, cybersecurity measures, and compliance with evolving regulations.

Training and transition specialists are pivotal in safeguarding the industry's workforce. Their expertise ensures that mariners are not left behind due to technological advancements but are empowered to operate autonomously, confidently, and competently. They are the conduits through which the industry's heritage blends seamlessly with its future, ensuring a harmonious transition into the era of autonomous shipping.

5. CYBERSECURITY EXPERTS

In the era of autonomous ships, where digital connectivity and data exchange are ubiquitous, the role of cybersecurity experts has emerged as indispensable. These highly specialised professionals are entrusted with the critical mission of fortifying the digital fortresses that safeguard onboard systems from the ever-evolving landscape of cyber threats.

The responsibilities of cybersecurity experts extend across a multifaceted spectrum. Their foremost concern is shielding autonomous vessels from cyberattacks, compromising safety, navigation, and data integrity. They employ advanced threat detection mechanisms and robust defence strategies to identify and thwart potential breaches. This includes safeguarding against malware, ransomware, and other malicious software that could infiltrate onboard systems.

Ensuring the integrity and confidentiality of data is another paramount task. The vast amounts of data generated and processed on autonomous ships, from navigation data to sensor readings, are critical to operational efficiency and sensitivity. Cybersecurity experts implement encryption, access controls, and data protection measures to prevent breaches and unauthorised access.

Furthermore, these professionals are tasked with continually evaluating and enhancing cybersecurity protocols to stay one step ahead of cyber adversaries. They are vigilant in identifying potential vulnerabilities and implementing proactive measures to fortify onboard systems against emerging threats. Cybersecurity experts are the digital guardians of autonomous ships, tirelessly working to ensure these advanced vessels' resilience, security, and reliability in an increasingly interconnected maritime landscape.

6. REMOTE OPERATIONS MANAGERS

The rise of remote operation centres has ushered in a pivotal role within the realm of autonomous ship management. that of the remote operations manager. These professionals are the orchestrators of maritime operations from afar, overseeing the central hubs that coordinate and supervise the intricate dance of autonomous vessels.

The responsibilities of remote operations managers encompass a wide array of critical functions. At the heart of their role is coordinating vessel operations, where they leverage real-time data and communication systems to ensure seamless navigation, cargo handling, and overall vessel performance. They work with autonomous vessel operators, data analysts, and technicians to meticulously watch vessel movements and activities.

In times of crisis or unforeseen events, remote operations managers are the calm and collected leaders who spring into action. They are responsible for initiating emergency response protocols, coordinating with relevant authorities, and making swift decisions to safeguard the vessel and its crew.

Safety is a paramount concern, and these managers are steadfast in ensuring that safety protocols are always followed. They are the guardians of compliance with maritime regulations, environmental standards, and industry best practices. In essence, they are the linchpin that ensures that the promise of autonomous shipping—enhanced safety, operational efficiency, and environmental responsibility—is upheld in practice.

Remote operations managers are pivotal in orchestrating autonomous ship management, crucial in advancing the industry's commitment to safe, efficient, and reliable autonomy. They embody the spirit of responsible oversight and seamless coordination in a maritime world where remote control centres are central to the future of shipping.

7. COLLABORATION FACILITATORS

In the dynamic landscape of autonomous shipping, collaboration becomes not just a preference but a necessity. Collaboration facilitators are professionals who foster cooperation and synergy among diverse stakeholders, including shipping companies, regulatory bodies, technology providers, and other key players. Their role is pivotal in ensuring the seamless integration of autonomous vessels into existing maritime operations.

Collaboration facilitators wear many hats. They act as intermediaries, bridging the gaps in understanding and communication that can often arise in multifaceted projects like autonomous ship deployment. They bring together industry experts, policymakers, and innovators to align their goals and visions, creating a unified front for the advancement of autonomous shipping.

One of their key responsibilities is to navigate the intricate web of regulations and standards that govern the maritime industry. They work closely with regulatory authorities to ensure that adopting autonomous vessels complies with evolving safety, security, and environmental standards. This involves facilitating dialogues, sharing insights, and contributing to developing regulatory frameworks that balance innovation and safety.

Furthermore, collaboration facilitators play a crucial role in fostering innovation and knowledge sharing. They facilitate partnerships and initiatives that drive the development of standardised approaches, best practices, and industry-wide solutions. Creating an environment conducive to collaboration ensures that autonomous shipping evolves sustainably and responsibly.

In essence, collaboration facilitators are the glue that holds together the diverse tapestry of autonomous shipping. Their expertise in building bridges, aligning interests, and driving consensus is essential for the industry's growth and success as it navigates the exciting but complex terrain of autonomy.

8. ADAPTATION AND LIFELONG LEARNING

In the ever-evolving landscape of the maritime industry, the call for adaptation and lifelong learning has never been more resonant. Maritime professionals find themselves in a dynamic environment where embracing adaptability and staying abreast of the latest technological advancements and regulatory changes is advantageous and essential.

The concept of adaptation extends beyond adopting new technology; it encompasses a mindset of continuous growth and improvement. Maritime professionals are increasingly required to cultivate this mindset as the industry undergoes rapid transformations driven by autonomous technology, digitalisation, and sustainability initiatives.

Lifelong learning becomes a cornerstone of success in this environment. Professionals must continue education and skill development to remain competitive and relevant. This may include specialised training in autonomous systems, cybersecurity, data analytics, or regulatory compliance.

Moreover, adaptation and lifelong learning are both individual endeavours and organisational imperatives. Shipping companies, regulatory bodies, and technology providers are embracing cultures of innovation and knowledge-sharing to keep pace with industry changes. Collaboration between industry stakeholders and educational institutions fosters research, development, and training programs that equip professionals with the skills needed to thrive in the maritime landscape of tomorrow.

Adaptation and lifelong learning are not merely responses to industry shifts; they are proactive strategies for staying agile, innovative, and resilient in a maritime world continually reshaped by technology, regulations, and sustainability goals.

9. HUMAN-MACHINE INTERACTION SPECIALISTS

In the intricate dance between humans and autonomous systems, specialists in human-machine interaction emerge as pivotal figures. Their expertise ensures the seamless and effective interaction between mariners and the autonomous technology that powers modern vessels.

The responsibilities of human-machine interaction specialists encompass a diverse range of tasks, all geared toward enhancing the interface between humans and autonomous systems. They design intuitive user interfaces that allow mariners to interact with onboard technology naturally and efficiently. These interfaces are engineered to be user-friendly, providing mariners with the tools and information to navigate the complexities of autonomous shipping easily.

Safety is a paramount concern in human-machine interaction. Specialists in this field focus on creating interfaces that facilitate communication and promote safety. They design systems that minimise cognitive load, allowing mariners to concentrate on their core responsibilities while entrusting autonomous systems with their designated tasks. Moreover, they ensure that user interfaces are designed with redundancies and fail-safe mechanisms, guaranteeing that mariners can intervene swiftly and effectively in unexpected events.

A profound understanding of human psychology and technological capabilities characterises the role of human-machine interaction specialists. They bridge the gap between mariners and autonomous technology, crafting interfaces and systems that foster trust, transparency, and effective collaboration. In this way, they contribute to the industry's commitment to safety, efficiency, and reliability in the realm of autonomous shipping.

10. SAFETY AND EMERGENCY RESPONSE EXPERTS

Safety is paramount in the maritime industry, and autonomous ships are no exception. The role of safety and emergency response experts is central to ensuring the well-being of crew members, the preservation of vessels, and the safeguarding of cargo in the face of unforeseen challenges and emergencies.

These professionals are well-versed in safety protocols, crisis management, and emergency response procedures tailored to the unique context of autonomous shipping. They work tirelessly to develop and implement comprehensive safety plans encompassing all aspects of vessel operation, from navigation and propulsion to cargo handling and communication systems.

Safety and emergency response experts are the calm and decisive leaders who guide crew members through crises. They oversee evacuation procedures, coordinate responses to fires, collisions, or other unforeseen events, and strictly follow safety protocols. Their expertise is invaluable in mitigating risks and minimising the impact of emergencies on both human life and maritime assets.

Furthermore, these experts collaborate closely with technology providers and vessel operators to develop and test emergency response scenarios for autonomous ships. They work to identify potential vulnerabilities, assess the robustness of safety systems, and refine protocols to adapt to the evolving nature of autonomy.

In essence, safety and emergency response experts are the guardians of maritime safety in the era of autonomous shipping. Their dedication to preparedness, proactive safety measures, and crisis management ensures that the industry prioritises safety and resilience as it embarks on the transformative journey of autonomy.

The evolution of maritime jobs and skill sets is a testament to the maritime industry's adaptability and resilience. As it embraces autonomy, the industry recognises that while technology can automate tasks, it cannot replace the irreplaceable human element—maritime expertise, experience, and adaptability. Consequently, the maritime professionals of tomorrow will not only navigate the seas but also the evolving technological landscape, ensuring a harmonious coexistence between tradition and innovation.

ENVIRONMENTAL BENEFITS AND SUSTAINABILITY

Adopting autonomous ships heralds a new era of environmental consciousness within the maritime industry. These vessels transform how goods are transported and significantly contribute to environmental sustainability. In this section, we explore the environmental benefits and sustainability aspects of autonomous shipping.

1. ROUTE OPTIMIZATION AND FUEL EFFICIENCY

Autonomous ships are heralding a new era of efficiency and sustainability in the maritime industry through route optimisation and fuel efficiency. At the heart of this transformation are advanced algorithms capable of optimising voyage routes with unparalleled precision. These algorithms consider many dynamic factors, including real-time weather conditions, ocean currents, and traffic patterns.

The result of this optimisation is not just improved navigation but a remarkable reduction in fuel consumption. By charting the most fuel-efficient courses, autonomous vessels minimise the energy required for propulsion, resulting in significant fuel savings. This, in turn, leads to a substantial reduction in greenhouse gas emissions, aligning the maritime industry with global efforts to combat climate change.

The impact of this efficiency extends far beyond individual voyages. As more autonomous ships join the global fleet, the cumulative effect on the maritime industry's carbon footprint is substantial. It represents a tangible step toward sustainable shipping practices, demonstrating the potential for the industry to reduce its environmental impact while improving operational efficiency significantly.

2. ECO-FRIENDLY HULL DESIGNS

In pursuing sustainability and reduced environmental impact, the maritime industry embraces innovative hull designs that are nothing short of eco-friendly marvels. These hull designs are not just aesthetically pleasing; they are engineered to reduce hydrodynamic resistance, a crucial factor in a vessel's overall fuel efficiency.

The secret lies in the meticulous engineering that goes into crafting these hulls. Their streamlined shapes are optimised to minimise drag as vessels move through the water. As a result, the energy required for propulsion is significantly reduced, translating into lower fuel consumption and, consequently, fewer emissions.

Beyond the immediate benefits of improved fuel efficiency, eco-friendly hull designs are a testament to the industry's commitment to sustainable practices. They represent a harmonious fusion of engineering ingenuity and environmental responsibility, showcasing the maritime sector's dedication to reducing its environmental footprint.

Moreover, these designs exemplify how autonomous shipping goes hand-in-hand with sustainability. As autonomous vessels evolve, they will increasingly leverage eco-friendly hulls, contributing to operational efficiency and a cleaner, greener future for the maritime industry and the planet.

3. ENERGY-EFFICIENT SYSTEMS

Within the heart of autonomous ships lies a commitment to energy efficiency that extends far beyond the propulsion system. These vessels are engineered with a holistic approach to onboard systems, where every component, from propulsion to lighting and HVAC (heating, ventilation, and air conditioning), is designed to prioritise energy conservation.

The propulsion systems of autonomous ships, for instance, are engineered for peak efficiency, minimising energy wastage and maximising energy conversion into forward motion. This meticulous engineering ensures that each drop of fuel or energy expended propels the vessel efficiently.

But the quest for energy efficiency continues beyond propulsion. Lighting systems use energy-saving technologies like LED lighting to reduce electricity consumption. HVAC systems are fine-tuned for optimal performance, maintaining comfortable onboard conditions while minimising energy expenditure. Every aspect of energy use is scrutinised and optimised to ensure that autonomous ships and their commitment to sustainable energy practices are autonomous in navigation.

The cumulative effect of these energy-efficient systems is a significant reduction in overall energy consumption during voyages. This translates into tangible benefits for the environment and operational costs, underlining the maritime industry's dedication to responsible and efficient autonomy.

4. REDUCED RISK OF OIL SPILLS

One of the most compelling advantages of autonomous ships is their remarkable capacity to reduce the risk of environmental disasters, particularly oil spills. At the core of this risk reduction is their advanced navigation systems and collision avoidance capabilities.

These autonomous vessels are equipped with cutting-edge technology to navigate precisely and safely. They can detect and assess potential collision risks well in advance, allowing for timely and proactive responses. This capability significantly minimises the likelihood of accidents that could lead to oil spills, which are both ecologically devastating and financially costly.

By taking a proactive approach to safety, autonomous ships exemplify a commitment to minimising the potential for catastrophic marine pollution. Their advanced sensors, real-time data analysis, and rapid decision-making capabilities contribute to a maritime world where environmental stewardship is at the forefront. This, in turn, aligns with the broader global goal of safeguarding our oceans and marine ecosystems from the detrimental effects of oil pollution.

In essence, the reduced risk of oil spills is a benefit of autonomy and a testament to the industry's dedication to responsible and safe shipping practices that protect our oceans and preserve their beauty for generations to come.

5. COMPLIANCE WITH EMISSION REGULATIONS

The maritime industry faces a growing imperative to reduce its environmental impact and comply with stringent emission regulations imposed by international and regional authorities. In this context, autonomous ships emerge as a beacon of compliance, well-positioned to meet these demanding standards.

At the heart of this compliance lies the remarkable reduction in emissions achieved by autonomous vessels. These ships significantly diminish their carbon footprint through route optimisation, energy-efficient systems, and eco-friendly hull designs. They consume less fuel, emit fewer greenhouse gases, and are highly committed to environmental sustainability.

By embracing autonomy, the maritime industry takes a substantial step toward aligning with global efforts to combat climate change and promote cleaner shipping practices. Autonomous ships contribute to a cleaner maritime industry, not merely as a byproduct of their operation but as a fundamental commitment to environmental stewardship.

The compliance achieved by autonomous ships extends beyond emissions reduction. Their advanced navigation and safety systems and proactive collision avoidance capabilities reduce the risk of accidents that could lead to environmental disasters. This proactive approach to safety minimises the potential for oil spills and other forms of marine pollution, further cementing their role in preserving the health of our oceans.

6. RENEWABLE ENERGY INTEGRATION

Some autonomous ships innovate by incorporating renewable energy sources into their design to pursue enhanced environmental sustainability. Solar panels and wind turbines become integral components of these vessels, contributing to onboard power generation and reducing reliance on traditional fossil fuels.

Integrating renewable energy sources represents a significant leap toward a more sustainable maritime industry. Solar panels, positioned strategically on the vessel's surface, harness the sun's power to generate electricity. Similarly, wind turbines, often mounted on masts or other high points of the ship, capture the energy of the wind and convert it into usable power.

The benefits of renewable energy integration are multifold. Firstly, it reduces the vessel's reliance on fossil fuels, diminishing emissions and carbon footprint. Next, it enhances energy efficiency, as the ship can utilise clean, renewable energy for various onboard systems. Finally, it aligns with global efforts to transition toward greener transportation solutions, contributing to a cleaner and more sustainable future for the maritime industry.

Autonomous ships that embrace renewable energy integration showcase a dedication to pushing the boundaries of environmental sustainability. They represent a harmonious synergy of technological innovation and ecological responsibility, forging a path toward cleaner and more eco-conscious maritime practices.

7. RESEARCH AND MONITORING

Autonomous ships are heralding a new era of scientific exploration and environmental monitoring on the high seas. These vessels are increasingly employed for various scientific research endeavours, spanning oceanography, marine biology, and environmental monitoring. Their autonomous capabilities enable them to serve as invaluable platforms for collecting valuable data on ocean conditions and marine ecosystems.

In oceanography, autonomous ships provide researchers with a unique vantage point for studying ocean currents, temperature variations, and marine life behaviours. These vessels can operate autonomously for extended periods, covering vast expanses of the ocean and gathering data that would be challenging or impossible to obtain through traditional research methods.

Marine biology benefits greatly from deploying autonomous ships, as they facilitate the study of marine species and their habitats in their natural environment. Researchers can leverage these vessels to conduct non-invasive observations, collect biological samples, and monitor the health of ecosystems. This wealth of data contributes to a deeper understanding of marine life and supports conservation efforts to protect vulnerable species and ecosystems.

Environmental monitoring is another key application of autonomous ships. These vessels are equipped with sensors and instruments capable of measuring a wide range of environmental parameters, from water quality and pollution levels to the presence of marine litter and the effects of climate change. By continuously collecting data on these factors, autonomous ships play a pivotal role in advancing our knowledge of marine environments and informing strategies for their preservation and sustainable management.

Autonomous ships have transcended their role as cargo carriers to become vital contributors to scientific research and environmental monitoring. They empower researchers and conservationists with the tools and capabilities to unravel the ocean's mysteries and safeguard its delicate ecosystems.

8. SUSTAINABLE PRACTICES

The shift toward autonomous shipping represents a technological transformation and a cultural shift within the maritime industry that encourages and champions sustainable practices. As the industry embraces autonomy, companies are not merely adopting environmentally friendly technologies but also promoting a holistic approach to eco-conscious behaviours and practices.

Reduced waste generation is a key pillar of this sustainability drive. Shipping companies are implementing waste reduction strategies, emphasising recycling, and minimising the generation of single-use plastics and other pollutants. Autonomous vessels are designed with waste management in mind, ensuring responsible disposal practices that minimise the environmental impact of maritime operations.

Responsible cargo handling is another facet of sustainable practices within the maritime industry. Autonomous ships are equipped with advanced cargo monitoring and security systems that minimise the risk of cargo damage, theft, or tampering. This ensures the safe transport of goods and reduces the potential for environmental harm in cargo-related incidents.

Adherence to international ballast water management standards is yet another dimension of sustainable practices promoted by autonomous shipping. These vessels incorporate ballast water treatment systems that prevent the transfer of invasive species between ecosystems, preserving the delicate balance of marine environments.

Summarily, the embrace of autonomous shipping goes beyond the realm of technology; it represents a cultural shift within the maritime industry that champions eco-conscious behaviours, responsible stewardship of the oceans, and a commitment to sustainability. Autonomous ships are not just vessels of commerce; they are beacons of a cleaner, greener maritime future.

9. INDUSTRY-WIDE COLLABORATION

In response to the escalating environmental concerns that loom over the maritime industry, a remarkable transformation is underway—an era of heightened collaboration among diverse stakeholders. This collaborative spirit has brought together shipping companies, technology providers, regulatory bodies, and environmental organisations in a united effort to address the industry's environmental impact and drive positive change.

At its core, industry-wide collaboration represents a shared commitment to sustainability and responsible stewardship of the oceans. Shipping companies, driven by the economic and environmental advantages offered by autonomous ships, are actively seeking solutions that minimise their carbon footprint and reduce emissions. They are partnering with technology providers to implement eco-friendly and innovative solutions that propel the industry toward a greener future.

Regulatory bodies are playing a pivotal role in shaping this collaborative landscape. They work closely with industry leaders to develop and refine regulations aligning with sustainability goals. By providing clarity, guidance, and a framework for compliance, these regulatory authorities facilitate the industry's transition toward cleaner and more environmentally responsible practices.

Environmental organisations bring an invaluable perspective to the table. They advocate for the preservation of marine ecosystems and advocate for sustainable practices. Through collaboration with industry stakeholders, they contribute to the development of responsible environmental initiatives, such as reducing marine litter and mitigating the impact of shipping on marine life.

This multifaceted collaboration extends beyond individual projects or initiatives; it represents a collective commitment to the broader cause of environmental preservation. It is a testament to the industry's recognition as a custodian of the oceans and its determination to work together to reduce its environmental impact.

Industry-wide collaboration is not just a response to environmental concerns; it is a proactive strategy for ushering in a maritime future that is cleaner, greener, and more sustainable. It embodies the collective determination to safeguard our oceans for generations to come.

The environmental benefits and sustainability aspects of autonomous shipping underscore its potential to drive positive change in the maritime industry. By embracing these vessels, the industry is taking significant steps toward reducing its environmental footprint, aligning with global sustainability goals, and ensuring that the world's oceans remain healthy and vibrant for generations.

ECONOMIC IMPLICATIONS

Integrating autonomous ships into the maritime industry carries profound economic implications that reshape the traditional dynamics of maritime transportation. While initial investments in autonomous technology can be substantial, the long-term economic benefits are substantial. Shipping companies find that reduced labour costs, increased operational efficiency, and minimised downtime translate into substantial savings over time. The ability of autonomous ships to operate 24/7 ensures the timely and efficient transport of goods, potentially boosting global trade.

However, there are also considerations regarding the economic impact on traditional maritime job sectors, which may face workforce challenges as automation advances. Nonetheless, the maritime industry recognises that adopting autonomous ships is a technological evolution and a strategic imperative for maintaining competitiveness in an increasingly globalised and dynamic marketplace. In this delicate balance between technological innovation and workforce adaptation, the true economic implications of autonomous shipping are unfolding.

Chapter 5

FUTURE TRENDS AND PROSPECTS

As the maritime industry navigates the transformative waters of autonomous shipping, the horizon is marked by future trends and prospects that promise to shape the course of this technological evolution. In this chapter, we embark on a journey to explore these trends and prospects, offering insights into what lies ahead for autonomous ships and their impact on the maritime landscape.

ADVANCEMENTS IN AUTONOMOUS SHIP TECHNOLOGIES

The relentless pursuit of innovation drives the evolution of autonomous ship technologies. As we look toward the horizon, several promising advancements are poised to shape the future of autonomous shipping.

1. ENHANCED AUTONOMY

One of the most compelling and transformative advancements is the journey toward enhanced autonomy for autonomous ships. Future vessels are set to feature highly advanced AI systems and cutting-edge algorithms that bestow them with the ability to make increasingly complex decisions autonomously. These decisions encompass many critical maritime tasks, ranging from intricate route planning to nimble collision avoidance strategies and even the adept adaptation to swiftly changing weather conditions.

This progression toward enhanced autonomy heralds a future where autonomous ships rely less on remote human intervention and become even more self-reliant. The vessels will evolve into entities that are not merely autonomous in name but truly autonomous in action, capable of navigating vast ocean expanses with precision and decision-making that rivals, if not, surpasses human capabilities. The result is a maritime industry where the bounds of autonomous operation are pushed to new limits, and the vessels themselves become increasingly adept captains of their destinies.

2. SENSOR TECHNOLOGY

Sensor technology is undergoing a rapid and transformative evolution, equipping autonomous ships with unprecedented situational awareness. Among the stars of this sensor technology revolution are LiDAR (Light Detection and Ranging) systems, advanced radar arrays, and state-of-the-art camera systems that collectively elevate a vessel's ability to understand and interpret its surroundings.

LiDAR, in particular, represents a quantum leap in autonomous ship technology. These laser-based sensors provide an incredibly detailed and real-time 3D map of the vessel's environment, allowing it to perceive and interact with the world around it in an unprecedented manner. Improved radar systems further enhance this situational awareness, precisely tracking nearby vessels, objects, and weather conditions. Advanced camera arrays with AI-driven image recognition bolster the ship's ability to detect and respond to obstacles with exceptional precision.

Combining these sensor technologies empowers autonomous ships to navigate with heightened confidence and safety. They can "see" and interpret their surroundings with remarkable clarity, enabling them to make split-second decisions that prioritise the safety of the vessel, its cargo, and the environment. This advancement enhances collision avoidance capabilities and ensures that autonomous ships can operate seamlessly in diverse maritime conditions.

3. AI AND MACHINE LEARNING

AI algorithms, in particular, will become more sophisticated, akin to the evolution of a ship's cognitive prowess. These algorithms will transcend their initial capabilities and grow into dynamic and adaptable systems. They will be able to learn from past experiences, equipping autonomous ships with the ability to accumulate knowledge and insights over time. This learning process will enable vessels to adapt swiftly to dynamic and ever-changing maritime environments.

One of the most remarkable outcomes of this advancement will be the vessel's capacity to make real-time decisions with unprecedented accuracy. AI algorithms will process a vast array of data, from onboard sensors to external sources, and synthesise this information to make swift, informed decisions. Whether it's adjusting course to avoid inclement weather, optimising propulsion for fuel efficiency, or managing complex navigation scenarios, AI-driven decision-making will further elevate safety and efficiency in autonomous shipping.

This synergy of AI and machine learning represents a profound shift in how autonomous ships operate. They won't merely adhere to predetermined routines; they will continuously learn, adapt, and refine their behaviours based on real-world experiences. The result is a maritime future where vessels are not just autonomous but highly intelligent, capable of navigating the complexities of the open sea with unprecedented precision and confidence.

4. CONNECTIVITY AND COMMUNICATION

In the autonomous shipping landscape of tomorrow, the connectivity and communication systems integrated into these vessels will stand as pillars of seamless interaction. Autonomous ships of the future will be equipped with cutting-edge communication systems that ensure unwavering connectivity, even in the most remote corners of the world's oceans.

These advanced communication systems will transcend the conventional boundaries of maritime connectivity, supporting real-time data exchange, remote monitoring, and coordinated interactions with other vessels and control centres. In essence, they will transform autonomous ships into beacons of interconnectedness in the vast expanse of the sea.

Real-time data exchange will be a convenience and a cornerstone of maritime operations. Autonomous ships will transmit information to and from control centres, providing crucial updates on their status, navigation, and environmental conditions. Remote monitoring will empower shore-based teams to oversee vessel operations, intervening when necessary and ensuring that safety and efficiency are maintained at the highest level.

Coordination with other vessels will become a seamless dance of communication as autonomous ships collaborate to navigate crowded waterways and respond to dynamic maritime scenarios. The result is a maritime world where autonomy is not synonymous with isolation but rather with unprecedented connectivity and collaboration.

5. CYBERSECURITY MEASURES

In the ever-evolving realm of autonomous shipping, the rising tide of digitalisation brings forth an imperative. The fortification of cybersecurity measures. As we gaze into the future, it becomes increasingly clear that safeguarding autonomous ships from the omnipresent spectre of cyber threats will be a paramount concern.

The autonomous vessels of tomorrow will be fortresses of digital defence, fortified by advanced cybersecurity protocols and technologies. These measures will serve as an impenetrable shield, ensuring onboard systems, data integrity, and safety. In a world where connectivity and data exchange are the lifeblood of maritime operations, protecting against cyber threats becomes not just a necessity but an unwavering commitment to maritime safety.

Future advancements in cybersecurity will encompass a spectrum of measures, from robust encryption and intrusion detection systems to advanced anomaly detection algorithms. These technologies will be woven into the fabric of autonomous ships, creating a digital bulwark that repels cyber threats with the same vigilance that traditional vessels navigate treacherous waters.

The importance of cybersecurity in autonomous shipping cannot be overstated. It is not merely a technical challenge but a pledge to protect the autonomy, safety, and data integrity of these vessels. As the digital frontier of autonomous shipping expands, so will the vigilance and sophistication of the security measures that stand guard.

6. HYBRID PROPULSION SYSTEMS

As the maritime industry charts a course toward a greener and more sustainable future, the prominence of hybrid propulsion systems comes into focus. These systems are poised to play a central role in enhancing fuel efficiency and reducing emissions within autonomous shipping.

Hybrid propulsion systems represent a convergence of tradition and innovation. They marry time-tested propulsion methods with alternative and eco-conscious energy sources, creating a synergy that powers the vessels of the future. The result is a maritime landscape where autonomous ships move forward with a reduced environmental footprint and a heightened commitment to sustainability.

These hybrid systems harness diverse energy sources, ranging from high-capacity batteries and hydrogen fuel cells to the elemental force of wind propulsion. By seamlessly integrating these sources into the vessel's propulsion architecture, autonomous ships are poised to reduce their reliance on traditional fossil fuels.

The benefits of hybrid propulsion are manifold. They translate into tangible reductions in greenhouse gas emissions and a substantial decrease in the maritime industry's carbon footprint. Additionally, they enhance the operational efficiency of autonomous vessels, contributing to reduced voyage durations and lower fuel consumption.

7. REMOTE DIAGNOSTICS AND PREDICTIVE MAINTENANCE

In the age of autonomous shipping, the synergy of technology and maritime expertise is most apparent in remote diagnostics and predictive maintenance. As we steer toward the future, autonomous ships are poised to embrace these cutting-edge technologies, transforming maintenance from a reactive necessity into a proactive and streamlined process.

The autonomous vessels of tomorrow will be equipped with advanced diagnostic tools that continually monitor the health and performance of onboard systems. With an arsenal of sensors and data analytics, these vigilant systems will act as vigilant sentinels, scrutinising every aspect of the ship's operation. Their mission is clear. They identified potential issues before they could escalate into costly and disruptive problems.

But the true marvel of this technological evolution is predictive maintenance. Autonomous ships will not merely diagnose issues; they will forecast them. Predictive maintenance systems will leverage data-driven insights to anticipate when components may require attention or replacement. These prescient systems will even go a step further, autonomously scheduling maintenance or repairs, ensuring they are executed precisely and with minimal disruption to operational schedules.

The result is a maritime landscape where downtime and operational disruptions become relics of the past. Autonomous ships will operate with unrivalled efficiency and reliability thanks to the tireless vigilance of remote diagnostics and predictive maintenance systems. These technologies are not just a glimpse of the future; they promise a maritime era where vessels are autonomous in their navigation and ability to maintain peak operational conditions.

8. ECO-FRIENDLY MATERIALS AND HULL DESIGNS

The eco-conscious ethos of autonomous shipping extends to the heart of vessel design, where integrating eco-friendly materials and innovative hull designs is set to revolutionise the maritime industry's environmental impact.

In the maritime landscape of the future, autonomous ships will be pioneers of sustainability. The vessels will be constructed meticulously, using eco-friendly materials that reduce their environmental footprint. These materials, ranging from recyclable composites to lightweight alloys, differ from conventional construction materials and offer significant benefits in reduced weight, increased durability, and enhanced fuel efficiency.

But it's not just the materials; the hull designs will bear innovation's hallmark. Autonomous ship design will prioritise hull shapes engineered for minimal hydrodynamic resistance, enabling vessels to glide effortlessly through the water with reduced energy consumption. These hulls will be a testament to the marriage of science and sustainability, epitomising a maritime industry committed to preserving our oceans.

The impact of these eco-friendly materials and hull designs is profound. They translate into tangible reductions in fuel consumption and greenhouse gas emissions, paving the way for a greener and more sustainable maritime future. Autonomous ships are not just vessels of commerce; they are ambassadors of environmental responsibility, guiding us toward a maritime era where sustainability is not an aspiration but a fundamental principle.

9. AUTONOMOUS FLEET MANAGEMENT

As we navigate into the future of autonomous shipping, the seascape will be adorned with the emergence of advanced fleet management systems. This transformational leap promises to reshape the very dynamics of maritime operations. These systems are poised to serve as the conductors of a symphony of autonomous vessels, orchestrating their movements and ensuring the maritime industry operates perfectly.

At the heart of this innovation lies the ability to coordinate the operations of multiple autonomous vessels within a single fleet. These advanced fleet management systems are akin to the maestros of the maritime world, choreographing a mesmerising ballet of ships that move with precision and efficiency. Their mission is multifaceted, encompassing the optimisation of routes, the meticulous management of cargo distribution, and the strategic deployment of the fleet's resources.

One of the cornerstones of this orchestration is route optimisation. Fleet management systems will harness a wealth of data, including weather conditions, traffic patterns, and real-time information from each vessel, to chart routes that are not just efficient but are a masterpiece of precision. These optimised routes will translate into substantial fuel savings, reduced voyage durations, and a greener ocean footprint.

But the magic doesn't end there. Cargo distribution will also fall under the purview of these systems. They will ensure that cargo is distributed strategically across the fleet, optimising stability and reducing the risk of imbalances. The result is a maritime world where cargo is not just transported but is a ballet of efficiency, with each vessel performing its part gracefully and precisely.

Efficient fleet deployment is the final crescendo in this maritime symphony. These systems ensure that vessels are dispatched strategically, responding to real-time demands and operational priorities. The result is a fleet that operates like a well-oiled machine, seamlessly adapting to the ebb and flow of maritime commerce.

The impact of autonomous fleet management is profound. It translates into reduced costs, enhanced operational efficiency, and a maritime industry that operates with the precision and grace of a ballet. As we venture further into the era of autonomous shipping, the role of these advanced fleet management systems will be nothing short of transformative, ensuring that the vessels of tomorrow navigate not just with autonomy but with the efficiency and elegance of a symphony.

As these advancements take shape, the autonomous ship technologies of tomorrow will not only redefine the capabilities of maritime transportation but also reaffirm the industry's commitment to innovation, safety, and sustainability. The horizon is brimming with possibilities, and the journey of autonomous shipping is a remarkable voyage into uncharted waters.

REGULATORY ADAPTATION AND STANDARDIZATION

The successful integration of autonomous ships into the maritime industry hinges on regulatory adaptation and standardisation. As we navigate this transformative era, several key developments are shaping the regulatory landscape and facilitating the coexistence of autonomy with established maritime norms.

1. INTERNATIONAL COLLABORATION

In the expansive seascape of autonomous shipping, the winds of change blow with a spirit of international collaboration. Maritime nations, recognising the transformative potential of autonomy, have embarked on collaborative efforts that transcend borders. This collective endeavour is driven by the shared vision of establishing unified standards that govern the realm of autonomous shipping, and the International Maritime Organization (IMO) stands at its helm.

The IMO, an eminent authority in the maritime world, has assumed a central role in shaping the future of autonomous shipping. This organisation, representing a multitude of nations, is working tirelessly to construct a regulatory framework that harmonises the diverse interests and aspirations of its member states. In doing so, it seeks to bridge the gaps and facilitate consensus on the rules and norms governing this rapidly evolving sector.

The essence of this international collaboration is the creation of a maritime landscape where autonomy is not a fragmented concept governed by disparate rules but a cohesive vision that transcends borders. The aim is to provide a level playing field for all nations and foster an environment where autonomous vessels can navigate with clarity and certainty, knowing they adhere to globally accepted standards.

2. FRAMEWORKS FOR AUTONOMOUS OPERATIONS

In the intricate tapestry of maritime regulation, a new chapter is being penned—a chapter that is dedicated to the specific nuances of autonomous ship operations. Mindful of autonomy's unique challenges and opportunities, regulatory authorities are crafting bespoke frameworks that address every facet of autonomous vessel conduct.

These frameworks clarify how autonomous ships should operate within the established maritime rules. Safety, the keystone of maritime regulations, finds prominence as these frameworks outline the measures and protocols that ensure the safe navigation of autonomous vessels. The guidance encompasses everything from navigation and collision avoidance to the meticulous handling of emergencies.

For the maritime industry, these frameworks represent more than just a set of rules; they are a compass that guides autonomous ships through the complexities of international waters. They offer the assurance that autonomy does not equate to ambiguity but to a structured and well-defined approach to maritime operations. Essentially, these frameworks are the heralds of a maritime future where autonomy and regulation walk hand in hand, ensuring that vessels navigate confidently and safely and adhere to the established norms.

3. SAFETY CERTIFICATION

In the evolving narrative of autonomous shipping, safety takes centre stage, and at its heart lies the concept of safety certification. As regulatory authorities adapt to the era of autonomy, they recognise that ensuring the safety of these advanced vessels requires a new paradigm—one that is characterised by stringent processes and meticulous scrutiny.

Safety certification for autonomous ships represents a rigorous evaluation process akin to a maritime crucible that these vessels must pass through. This process is designed to validate that autonomous ships adhere to stringent safety standards, leaving no room for compromise. It encompasses many facets, each meticulously examined to ensure the highest level of safety.

At the forefront of safety certification are cybersecurity measures. In an age where digital connectivity is ubiquitous, ensuring the integrity and security of onboard systems is paramount. Autonomous ships must demonstrate robust cybersecurity measures that safeguard against cyber threats, intrusions, and data breaches. These measures are not just checkboxes; they are the bulwarks that protect these vessels and the oceans they traverse.

Fail-safe mechanisms, another cornerstone of safety certification, are the safety nets that autonomous ships must possess. These mechanisms are designed to anticipate and respond to unforeseen circumstances or emergencies. They are the guardians of autonomy, ensuring it is swift and effective when human intervention is required.

Safety certification represents the uncompromising commitment of regulatory authorities to maritime safety in the autonomous age. It is the assurance that autonomy is not synonymous with recklessness but is a structured and vigilant approach to maritime operations. In essence, safety certification is the lighthouse that guides autonomous ships through the complexities of regulation and ensures they navigate with the highest safety standards.

4. LIABILITY AND INSURANCE GUIDELINES

In the intricate dance of regulatory adaptation, one of the most challenging steps is addressing the questions of liability and insurance in the context of autonomous shipping. As the maritime industry embraces autonomy, it grapples with the need for clear, comprehensive guidelines that determine responsibility and mitigate risk.

Liability guidelines are the compass that navigates the labyrinth of accountability in the event of accidents involving autonomous ships. They are designed to clarify who bears responsibility when unforeseen circumstances unfold. These guidelines encompass a range of scenarios, from collisions to equipment failures, ensuring that accountability is not a vague concept but a well-defined principle.

Insurance models, too, are undergoing a metamorphosis to align with the unique risks associated with autonomous operations. These models must factor in the complexities of autonomy, including cybersecurity risks, system failures, and the role of human intervention. They must provide comprehensive coverage that safeguards shipping companies and instils confidence in the industry's stakeholders.

Addressing liability and insurance considerations is a legal exercise and a vital element in the maritime industry's adaptation to autonomy. These guidelines assure that in the event of unforeseen challenges, a framework is in place to determine responsibility and provide compensation. They are the safeguard that ensures that the transition to autonomy is not just a technological leap but a responsible and well-regulated evolution of maritime operations.

5. OPERATIONAL TRANSPARENCY

In the symphony of autonomous shipping regulation, operational transparency plays a harmonious and essential note. Regulatory authorities, with their watchful eyes on the maritime horizon, recognise the importance of real-time insights into the operations of autonomous vessels. This emphasis on transparency is a testament to the commitment to safety and accountability that underpins the regulatory landscape.

Operational transparency requires autonomous ships to provide a continuous stream of real-time data—a digital heartbeat that pulses with information about their status, location, and intended routes. This data, akin to a maritime logbook of the digital age, serves a dual purpose. It enhances situational awareness for maritime authorities, offering them an unobstructed view of the movements and conditions of autonomous vessels traversing the seas under their jurisdiction.

But transparency is not solely about oversight; it is also a mechanism for ensuring compliance with navigation rules and regulations. Autonomous ships equipped with an array of sensors and advanced systems must demonstrate adherence to established norms. They must navigate in accordance with the rules of the sea, avoiding collisions, respecting traffic patterns, and responding to emergencies with precision.

Operational transparency is the cornerstone of a maritime era where autonomy is not synonymous with opacity but with clarity. It is the promise that the digital veins of autonomous ships are open to scrutiny, ensuring that these vessels operate with the transparency and accountability that are the hallmarks of a safe and responsible maritime industry.

6. TRAINING AND CERTIFICATION STANDARDS

In the grand tapestry of autonomous shipping, the importance of well-prepared human hands on the digital helm cannot be overstated. Regulatory authorities, cognizant of this fact, are diligently crafting training and certification standards that guide the preparation of personnel responsible for autonomous ship operations.

These standards are a roadmap to competence, encompassing the skills, knowledge, and expertise required to manage and monitor autonomous vessels effectively. They recognise that autonomy does not diminish the role of maritime personnel but transforms it into one requiring proficiency in traditional seamanship and cutting-edge technology.

The training and certification standards are the architects of competence, outlining the curricula and requirements for maritime personnel who step into the world of autonomy. They encompass a spectrum of subjects, from understanding the intricacies of autonomous systems to mastering the nuances of remote monitoring and control. These standards leave no room for ambiguity; they are the yardstick that measures readiness.

But these standards are not just for individuals but also a testament to the maritime industry's commitment to safety and excellence. They ensure that autonomous ship personnel do so with the knowledge and expertise to navigate the seas with precision and responsibility.

In training and certification standards, autonomy does not represent a reduction in rigour but a transformation in the skill set required. These standards assure that the human element in autonomous shipping is not just a cog in the digital machinery but a well-prepared and competent guardian of the seas.

7. CONTINUOUS REVIEW AND ADAPTATION

In the ever-evolving landscape of autonomous shipping, regulation is not a static monolith but a living, breathing organism that must adapt to the changing tides of technology and industry. Regulatory bodies, keenly aware of the dynamic nature of this realm, have committed themselves to a principle of continuous review and adaptation. This commitment embodies the spirit of agility and foresight.

This commitment is a recognition that the pace of technological advancement is relentless. Autonomous ship technologies are in a perpetual state of evolution, marked by innovations, enhancements, and unforeseen challenges. In this environment, regulations are not etched in stone but are documents that must remain responsive to the shifting sands of progress.

Regulatory bodies serve as the vigilant guardians of the maritime industry, ready to update and refine standards as autonomous ship technologies evolve. They embrace a mindset that is not just reactive but proactive—a mindset that anticipates the needs and challenges of the future. This forward-looking approach ensures that regulations remain effective in safeguarding safety, security, and the environment.

Continuous review and adaptation are the pillars of a regulatory framework that does not just keep pace with technology but sets the course for its responsible and safe integration into the maritime industry. It is the promise that in the autonomous era, regulation is not a constraint but an enabler—an enabler that fosters innovation while upholding the values and principles that underpin maritime operations.

8. PUBLIC ENGAGEMENT

In the era of autonomous shipping, the sails of regulation are not just steered by authorities but are propelled by the winds of public opinion and stakeholder perspectives. Regulatory bodies, recognising the importance of trust and acceptance, have made public engagement a cornerstone of their approach—inviting dialogue, discourse, and shared decision-making.

Public engagement is the open door through which regulatory authorities welcome the public's and stakeholders' voices into the regulatory process. It is a recognition that autonomy is not just a technological transformation but a societal one, touching upon ethical, safety, and environmental aspects that resonate with a wide spectrum of interests.

Through public engagement, regulatory bodies foster transparency and inclusivity. They ensure that all perspectives are considered, from maritime professionals' concerns to environmental advocates' aspirations. They create forums for dialogue on the ethical dimensions of autonomy, the safety implications, and the environmental impacts.

This engagement is not a token gesture but a commitment to building trust and acceptance. It assures that regulation is not a closed-door affair but a collaborative endeavour. In the age of autonomy, public engagement ensures that the regulatory compass is set not just by authorities but by society's collective wisdom and aspirations—a compass that guides autonomous ships on a course that is responsible, ethical, and embraced by all.

9. COLLABORATION WITH INDUSTRY

In the intricate dance of regulatory adaptation, a harmonious partnership takes centre stage—a partnership forged through collaboration between regulatory bodies and industry stakeholders. This collaboration is the lifeblood of successful regulatory adaptation, and it exemplifies a shared commitment to shape regulations that are both effective and responsive to the evolving landscape of autonomy.

Shipping companies, technology providers, and research institutions are at the heart of this collaboration—the protagonists of the maritime industry's transformation. These stakeholders are not passive observers of regulation but active participants who bring their expertise, insights, and experiences to the regulatory table.

Shipping companies provide a pragmatic perspective with their intimate knowledge of operational challenges and commercial imperatives. They articulate the real-world implications of regulation on maritime operations, ensuring that standards align with industry needs.

Technology providers, the architects of autonomy, offer invaluable insights into the capabilities and limitations of autonomous systems. They bring a technological lens to regulation, helping craft standards that reflect autonomy's cutting-edge possibilities and challenges.

Research institutions, the crucibles of innovation, contribute to the regulatory dialogue with a forward-looking perspective. They explore emerging technologies, identify potential risks, and offer solutions that anticipate future needs.

This collaboration is not a mere exchange of ideas but a collective effort to balance safety, innovation, and efficiency. It ensures that regulations are not just theoretical constructs but practical guidelines that enhance the safety and sustainability of maritime operations.

Collaboration with industry is a testament to the maritime industry's resilience and adaptability. It embodies a regulatory framework that embraces the wisdom and insights of those charting the course to autonomy. In this partnership, autonomy is a technological shift and a collaborative journey towards a safer, more efficient, and responsible maritime future.

As regulatory adaptation and standardisation efforts progress, they provide the maritime industry with the framework to confidently embrace autonomous shipping. This collaborative endeavour seeks to strike a delicate balance between innovation and safety, ensuring that autonomous ships can seamlessly integrate into existing maritime operations while upholding the highest standards of maritime safety and security.

EXPANSION OF AUTONOMOUS SHIP OPERATIONS

The trajectory of autonomous ship operations is marked by a compelling narrative of expansion, where the boundaries of maritime transportation are redefined, and new horizons are explored. This section explores the factors contributing to the widening operational scope of autonomous vessels.

1. DIVERSE VESSEL TYPES

The canvas of autonomous ship operations is a tapestry of diversity, with vessel types spanning a wide spectrum of functions and applications. This multifaceted expansion of autonomous vessels is akin to an orchestra, with each vessel type playing a distinct tune in the maritime symphony.

At the forefront of this diversification are cargo carriers, the workhorses of global trade. Autonomous cargo vessels are revolutionising the logistics and shipping industry, offering efficiency gains, reduced operational costs, and adherence to precise schedules. These ships navigate the open seas with the precision of digital maestros, optimising routes and cargo distribution to maximise efficiency.

But the cast of autonomous vessels doesn't stop at cargo carriers. Specialised research vessels equipped with advanced sensors and data-gathering capabilities venture into the uncharted waters of marine science. They collect invaluable data on ocean conditions, marine life, and environmental parameters, contributing to our understanding of the world's oceans and supporting conservation efforts.

The maritime stage also welcomes offshore platforms, where autonomous vessels participate in offshore oil and gas exploration and renewable energy projects. These ships conduct delicate manoeuvres near oil rigs and wind farms, demonstrating their prowess in environments where human presence can be perilous.

From container ships to research vessels to offshore platforms, autonomous ships embrace diverse roles in the maritime opera. Their ability to adapt to various functions not only broadens the scope of maritime applications but also unlocks new possibilities for industries that rely on the seas for their operations.

2. REMOTE AND HAZARDOUS OPERATIONS

The rise of autonomous ships is the dawn of a new era in conducting remote and hazardous operations, where the role of human crews is reimagined, and the limits of maritime exploration are pushed to new extremes.

These vessels are the intrepid explorers of the oceans, charting courses through remote and challenging environments. One such arena is the Arctic, where autonomous ships navigate ice-covered waters with precision and safety. In this inhospitable region, they conduct scientific research, monitor environmental changes, and support shipping operations, all while reducing the risks to human life.

Offshore wind farms, poised to become a major renewable energy source, welcome autonomous vessels as their guardians. These ships perform intricate tasks such as installing, maintaining, and inspecting wind turbines. In the swaying seas, they showcase their ability to work tirelessly, unaffected by fatigue or adverse conditions.

In offshore oil and gas exploration, autonomous vessels are the sentinels of the deep. They survey underwater structures, monitor pipelines, and conduct delicate operations around drilling platforms. Their precision and adaptability reduce risks and enhance safety in this demanding sector.

Expanding autonomous ship operations into remote and hazardous realms is not just about efficiency and cost-effectiveness; it's about ensuring the safety of human lives and preserving the delicate ecosystems of these environments. Autonomous vessels are the vanguards of exploration, pushing the boundaries of what is possible in the maritime world and opening new frontiers in human understanding and industry.

3. EFFICIENT PORT OPERATIONS

The influence of autonomous technology in reshaping maritime operations extends its reach to the gateways of global trade—ports and harbours. In these bustling hubs of commerce, automation is the harbinger of enhanced efficiency, streamlined logistics, and a revolution in port management.

Imagine a modern port where autonomous cargo-handling equipment dances in choreographed precision. Giant cranes swing into action, plucking containers from stacks with robotic grace. Unmanned transport vehicles shuttle goods from ship to shore and through the labyrinthine maze of storage yards. Every movement, every action, is a testament to efficiency.

This transformation is not confined to container terminals alone; it extends to the waterfront. The era of pilotless tugboats has dawned, as autonomous vessels seamlessly guide massive container ships and tankers into berths. These workhorses of the harbour no longer require a human hand at the helm. Instead, they are guided by algorithms and sensors, executing manoeuvres with digital finesse.

This autonomous revolution in port operations results in a symphony of productivity. Ports become beacons of efficiency, where cargo flows with clockwork precision, and time and space constraints are transcended. Loading and unloading have become rapid and cost-effective, reducing turnaround times for vessels and enabling the swift exchange of goods on a global scale.

4. MARITIME CONNECTIVITY

In the boundless expanse of the ocean, connectivity has traditionally been a challenge. Yet, in the age of autonomy, even the remotest corners of the maritime world are woven into a web of seamless communication.

Imagine an autonomous vessel, far from shore, sailing through the open ocean. Its isolation is an illusion, for it is tethered to a digital lifeline that connects it to control centres, fellowships, and the global maritime network.

Advanced communication systems are the architects of this connectivity. Autonomous ships maintain continuous contact with control centres, sharing real-time data on their status, location, and operational parameters. These control centres provide guidance, monitor performance, and intervene when necessary, all from the comfort of land-based operations rooms.

This connectivity extends beyond the vessel, reaching out to nearby ships. Autonomous vessels communicate with one another, sharing information about their courses, speeds, and intentions. They collaborate, navigating busy sea lanes with coordinated precision that minimises the risk of collisions and ensures safe passage.

Even in the remotest regions of the ocean, where once the void of isolation reigned supreme, maritime connectivity prevails. Autonomous ships are never truly alone, for they are part of a digital ecosystem that spans the seas. They are interconnected, data-driven, and equipped to confront the challenges of the open ocean with the assurance of constant communication.

Maritime connectivity is more than a technological achievement; it is the lifeline that binds the maritime world into a cohesive, responsive, and interconnected whole. In the era of autonomy, even the ocean's vastness is not a barrier but a conduit for global maritime operations.

5. MARITIME RESEARCH AND EXPLORATION

The advent of autonomous ships has redrawn the horizon of maritime research and exploration. These vessels are not just tools; they are pioneering partners in unravelling the secrets of the world's oceans, conducting studies that deepen our understanding of marine ecosystems, uncover the mysteries of the deep, and propel the frontiers of science.

Once constrained by human limitations, oceanographic expeditions now set sail with autonomous vessels as their companions. These ships are equipped with a treasure trove of sensors and instruments, from sonar systems to deep-sea sensors, capable of collecting data with unrivalled precision. They delve into the ocean's depths, mapping its contours, measuring its currents, and deciphering its mysteries.

Marine biology research leaps forward with autonomous ships. Scientists study marine life with underwater cameras and acoustic sensors, from the tiniest plankton to majestic whales. These vessels enable researchers to conduct long-term, uninterrupted observations, shedding light on the behaviours and migration patterns of aquatic species.

Beneath the waves, autonomous underwater vehicles (AUVs) play the role of explorers, descending into the abyss to unravel secrets hidden in the depths. These robotic companions survey shipwrecks, explore hydrothermal vents and gather samples from the ocean floor. They provide access to realms previously beyond human reach, expanding our knowledge of the ocean's geology and biology.

Maritime research and exploration, once the realm of intrepid adventurers, now have a technological ally. Autonomous ships enable scientists to push the boundaries of knowledge, unlock the sea's mysteries, and deepen our appreciation of the planet's most enigmatic and abundant ecosystem—the ocean.

6. UNMANNED CARGO TRANSPORTATION

The logistics industry is at the cusp of a transformative revolution, where the movement of goods no longer relies on the hands of human operators alone. Unmanned cargo transportation systems are emerging as a formidable force, offering a seamless, end-to-end solution for the efficient and cost-effective transport of goods.

In this logistics ecosystem, autonomous ships take centre stage as the maritime carriers of tomorrow. They sail the seas precisely, efficiently carrying goods from port to port, surpassing human crews. These vessels optimise routes, manage cargo distribution, and adhere to schedules with digital prowess, ensuring the timely delivery of goods to global markets.

But the autonomy doesn't stop at sea. Drones take flight from autonomous ships, delivering cargo to remote locations, surveying maritime environments, and bridging the last mile of logistics. They soar above the waves, expanding the reach of cargo transport to coastal and island communities and remote offshore installations.

Autonomous delivery vehicles navigate urban streets on land, ensuring that goods reach their final destinations swiftly and safely. These ground-based robots traverse cityscapes precisely, delivering packages to doorsteps and businesses without human intervention.

Unmanned cargo transportation is not just a technological evolution but a logistical revolution. It streamlines supply chains, reduces operational costs, and optimises the global movement of goods. In the era of autonomy, cargo transport is not just efficient; it is a symphony of automation that harmonises logistics in maritime, aerial, and terrestrial realms.

7. CUSTOMIZATION AND ADAPTABILITY

The era of autonomy brings a new paradigm in vessel design. In this era, ships are not just standard templates but adaptable platforms, ready to evolve to meet the unique demands of diverse missions. This customizability and adaptability are redefining the very essence of maritime operations.

Autonomous ship technology is the architect behind this transformation. These vessels are designed with modularity, featuring interchangeable equipment and configurable layouts. This modular approach allows ships to shed their one-size-fits-all identity and embrace versatility.

Imagine an autonomous vessel that starts its life as a cargo carrier, efficiently transporting goods across the seas. But then, the call comes for a scientific expedition, a mission to study ocean currents or survey the seabed. In a matter of days, this vessel transforms, shedding its cargo holds and equipping itself with the tools of scientific inquiry. It becomes a floating research platform, ready to unlock the mysteries of the deep.

The adaptability of autonomous ships extends to offshore operations. An oil rig requires maintenance, an underwater pipeline needs inspection, or an offshore wind farm demands servicing. Autonomous vessels rise to the occasion, adjusting their configurations and deploying specialised equipment to fulfil their new roles.

This flexibility is a testament to technological innovation and a boon for industries and organisations that rely on maritime assets. Autonomous vessels can be tailored to suit specific missions, whether surveying the ocean floor, assisting in search and rescue operations, or conducting environmental monitoring.

The age of customisation and adaptability in maritime operations is here. Autonomous ships stand ready to embrace each mission's unique challenges and opportunities, proving that in the era of autonomy, the seas are not just highways but a canvas for innovation.

8. MARITIME SERVICES

Autonomous vessels are not confined to the role of cargo carriers; they are multifaceted contributors to the broader maritime ecosystem. Beyond the transportation of goods, they offer a diverse range of specialised services that span the realms of exploration, conservation, and safety.

Consider the role of autonomous ships in seabed mapping. Equipped with advanced sonar systems and deep-sea sensors, these vessels serve as roving cartographers of the ocean floor. They create intricate maps that unveil the mysteries of underwater landscapes, aiding in scientific research, resource exploration, and environmental protection.

Environmental monitoring is another facet of their contribution. Autonomous vessels are equipped with sensors that can detect changes in water quality, monitor marine ecosystems, and track the movements of marine life. They provide valuable data for research, conservation efforts, and early warning systems for environmental disasters.

Autonomous ships become the unsung heroes of search and rescue operations in times of distress. They can swiftly deploy remotely operated vehicles (ROVs) to search for missing vessels, monitor disaster-stricken areas, and assist in recovering critical resources.

Offshore maintenance is yet another domain where these vessels shine. Oil rigs, wind farms, and underwater pipelines require periodic inspection and servicing. With their adaptability and specialised equipment, autonomous ships are ideally suited to tackle these tasks efficiently and safely.

The realm of maritime services is expanding thanks to the versatility and capability of autonomous vessels. They are not just vessels but enablers of exploration, guardians of the environment, and beacons of safety on the high seas. In the maritime ecosystem, their contributions are as varied as the ocean itself.

9. TOURISM AND LEISURE

The world of tourism and leisure is undergoing a sea change, and at its helm are the elegant autonomous cruise ships, offering passengers a remarkable journey across the oceans, all while redefining the concept of maritime travel.

Imagine embarking on a voyage on one of these modern marvels, where the focus is on the destination and the journey itself. Autonomous cruise ships epitomise luxury, combining the opulence of traditional cruise liners with the cutting-edge technology of autonomy.

As you board, you are greeted by a world of comfort and sophistication. These vessels are designed with the utmost attention to detail, featuring spacious cabins with panoramic ocean views, world-class dining options, and entertainment venues that rival those of top resorts. It's a floating paradise where every amenity is tailored to give passengers an unforgettable experience.

But their commitment to sustainability sets these autonomous cruise ships apart. They are eco-conscious vessels that embrace a green approach to maritime travel. Advanced propulsion systems, energy-efficient technologies, and eco-friendly practices minimise their environmental footprint, ensuring that your journey doesn't come at the planet's expense.

As you traverse the open seas, you'll witness breathtaking vistas, from serene sunsets on the horizon to encounters with marine life that only the ocean can offer. And while indulging in the luxurious offerings on board, you'll have the peace of mind that your voyage contributes to a more sustainable future for maritime tourism.

Autonomous cruise ships are not just vessels but gateways to a new maritime exploration and leisure era. They embody the perfect blend of technology and luxury, immersing passengers in the ocean's wonders while treading lightly on the environment. In maritime tourism, they are the vanguard of a remarkable voyage.

The expansion of autonomous ship operations signifies a new era in maritime transportation, where technology transcends boundaries and unlocks unattainable opportunities. As autonomous vessels venture into diverse applications and environments, they are poised to reshape how goods are transported, research is conducted, and global trade is facilitated. This expansion underscores the limitless potential of autonomous shipping to transcend the limits of conventional maritime operations.

SUSTAINABILITY AND GREEN INITIATIVES IN AUTONOMOUS SHIPPING

Sustainability is a cornerstone of the autonomous shipping revolution, underpinned by a resolute commitment to green initiatives to reduce maritime operations' environmental footprint significantly. A series of pivotal sustainability measures takes centre stage in this transformative landscape, steering autonomous vessels toward a more eco-conscious future.

Integrating renewable energy sources into the heart of autonomous ships is at the forefront of these initiatives. Solar panels, wind turbines, and cutting-edge hydrogen fuel cells are in the vessels' propulsion systems. These renewable energy solutions represent more than technological advancements; they symbolise a departure from traditional fossil fuel reliance and a substantial reduction in greenhouse gas emissions.

In tandem with the shift towards renewable energy, autonomous ships boast innovative, energy-efficient designs. These designs are more than aesthetic; they reflect a holistic approach encompassing eco-friendly hull shapes and energy-efficient onboard systems. Such designs optimise fuel consumption, minimise harmful emissions, and bolster overall energy efficiency, all while ensuring that vessel performance remains at the peak of maritime excellence.

Moreover, sustainability initiatives encompass a concerted drive to reduce emissions. Autonomous ships harness emission reduction technologies with vigour. These technologies include exhaust gas cleaning systems (commonly known as scrubbers) and selective catalytic reduction (SCR) mechanisms, each working diligently to mitigate the emission of pollutants, such as sulfuric oxides (SOx) and nitrogen oxides (NOx), into the atmosphere.

Ballast water management, a critical environmental stewardship component, receives careful attention in autonomous shipping. These vessels adhere to stringent ballast water management standards, meticulously designed to prevent the inadvertent spread of invasive species. These standards are not mere regulations but a testament to the commitment to preserving the ecological balance of marine ecosystems.

Simultaneously, autonomous ships embrace eco-friendly materials that have minimal ecological impact. Sustainable composites and coatings are increasingly employed in construction to reduce biofouling, ensuring enhanced fuel efficiency and reducing the vessel's ecological footprint.

Waste reduction and recycling take centre stage in the commitment to sustainability. Autonomous ships are equipped with advanced waste management systems, efficiently processing and recycling waste materials, which minimises disposal at sea and aligns with responsible waste management practices.

An integral part of sustainability lies in the active role that autonomous ships play in environmental monitoring and research. Equipped with sensors and data collection systems, these vessels actively contribute to scientific endeavours, studying ocean conditions, monitoring marine life, and advancing our understanding of climate change impacts on marine ecosystems.

The industry's commitment to sustainability is further fortified through collaborations with environmental organisations. These partnerships are pivotal in implementing and championing sustainable practices, reducing the impact of shipping on delicate marine environments, and ensuring the responsible operation of autonomous vessels.

Ambitious carbon neutrality goals set the tone for a sustainable, green future in autonomous shipping. These efforts encompass comprehensive strategies to offset carbon emissions, often involving investments in carbon capture technologies, reforestation projects, and participation in carbon trading mechanisms.

In the ever-evolving world of autonomous shipping, sustainability and green initiatives stand as guiding stars, setting a new course for the maritime industry—one that embodies ecological responsibility, the preservation of marine ecosystems, and the unwavering commitment to ensuring that the world's oceans remain vibrant and thriving for generations to come.

The future of autonomous shipping is a canvas on which technological ingenuity, regulatory cooperation, and environmental stewardship converge. The trends and prospects outlined in this chapter paint a compelling picture of an agile, sustainable, and technologically advanced maritime industry. As we set sail into this future, the transformative power of autonomy is poised to reshape the maritime landscape and our perceptions of what is possible on the open seas.

Chapter **6**

SAFETY AND ETHICAL CONSIDERATIONS

In the journey toward widespread adoption of autonomous ships, addressing critical safety and ethical considerations is imperative. This chapter delves into the heart of these concerns, offering insights into the ethical questions surrounding autonomous ships, the safety protocols and fail-safe mechanisms that underpin their operation, and the public perception and acceptance of this transformative technology.

ETHICAL QUESTIONS SURROUNDING AUTONOMOUS SHIPS

The advent of autonomous ships is a technological leap and a realm fraught with ethical considerations that demand contemplation and deliberation. As these vessels navigate the open seas, they navigate a complex web of ethical questions with far-reaching implications.

1. Moral Responsibility in Ethical Dilemmas. Autonomous ships must grapple with ethical dilemmas like their autonomous vehicle counterparts. Questions arise about how these vessels should make decisions when faced with challenging moral choices. For instance, in situations where a collision is imminent, should autonomous ships prioritise the safety of their passengers or act in the best interest of minimising overall harm, even if it means endangering those on board?

2. Programming Ethical Decision-Making. Programming autonomous decision-making algorithms introduces another layer of ethical complexity. The creators and programmers of these algorithms must make choices about what ethical principles and priorities should guide the ship's actions. This begs the question of whose ethical values should be embedded in the algorithms and how to address potential bias in these decisions.

3. Accountability for Accidents. Accidents are unfortunate in any transportation system, and autonomous ships are no exception. Ethical concerns encompass issues of accountability. Who is responsible when an accident involving an autonomous ship occurs? Is it the vessel's operator, the technology provider, or a combination of stakeholders? Addressing these concerns is pivotal in ensuring justice and accountability in maritime accidents.

4. Data Privacy and Security. The collection and sharing of vast data for autonomous operations raises ethical questions about data privacy and security. How should autonomous ships handle and protect the data they collect, including sensitive information about cargo, routes, and environmental conditions? Ensuring data privacy and safeguarding against cyber threats is a moral obligation in the digital age.

5. Ethical Considerations in Autonomous Warfare. Beyond civilian applications, autonomous ships are also used in military contexts. Ethical concerns emerge regarding using autonomous vessels in warfare, particularly the potential for reduced human oversight in combat scenarios and the moral implications of autonomous weaponry.

As the maritime industry embraces autonomy, these ethical questions call for careful consideration and ethical frameworks prioritising safety, fairness, and the well-being of humans and the marine environment. By addressing these questions, the industry can navigate towards a future where autonomous ships bring technological advancement and uphold ethical standards that align with our societal values.

SAFETY PROTOCOLS AND FAIL-SAFE MECHANISMS

Safety is the bedrock of the autonomous shipping industry. Ensuring the well-being of crew, cargo, and the marine environment is paramount. To achieve this, a comprehensive framework of safety protocols and fail-safe mechanisms has been meticulously woven into the fabric of autonomous shipping.

- Advanced Collision Avoidance Systems. Autonomous ships are equipped with state-of-the-art collision avoidance systems that transcend the capabilities of traditional maritime navigation. These systems leverage advanced sensors, radar, LiDAR (Light Detection and Ranging), and real-time data processing to provide an unparalleled awareness of the vessel's surroundings. They detect potential collision risks and make split-second decisions to avoid them. The result is a reduced likelihood of accidents, such as collisions with other ships, structures, or marine life.

- Real-Time Monitoring and Data Analysis. The cornerstone of safety in autonomous shipping is real-time monitoring and data analysis. These vessels have sensors that continuously collect information about the ship's performance, environmental conditions, and potential hazards. Advanced algorithms analyse this data in real time, flagging anomalies or potential issues. In case of irregularities, the vessel can automatically adjust its course, speed, or operational parameters to maintain safety. This proactive approach minimises the risk of accidents due to unforeseen circumstances.

- Contingency and Emergency Response Plans. Autonomous ships are prepared for various scenarios. They feature meticulously crafted contingency and emergency response plans that cover various possible incidents, from equipment failures to environmental emergencies. These plans define procedures for the crew or remote operators to follow in case of unforeseen events. Fail-safe mechanisms automatically engage when an emergency is detected, and the ship can take actions such as shutting down specific systems, activating emergency propulsion, or deploying life-saving equipment.

- Standardised Safety Guidelines. The maritime industry recognises the need for standardised safety guidelines for autonomous ships. These guidelines ensure that all autonomous vessels adhere to the same safety protocols, minimising the risk of accidents due to inconsistencies in operation. They address various safety aspects, including collision avoidance, navigation rules, equipment redundancy, and safety certifications. These standards serve as the foundation for safe, autonomous shipping.

- Incorporation of Cybersecurity Measures. In an era where cyber threats are a persistent concern, cybersecurity measures are integrated into autonomous ships to safeguard against digital intrusions. These measures protect the ship's onboard systems from hacking or malicious interference, ensuring that critical navigation, propulsion, and safety systems remain immune to external attacks.

- Design with Redundancy. Autonomous vessels are designed with redundancy in mind. Critical systems, such as navigation, propulsion, and communication, are duplicated to ensure that the ship can continue operating even during system failures. Redundancy extends to power systems, where backup generators or energy sources ensure the ship remains operational, particularly in emergencies.

- Crisis Management Training. Crew members and remote operators receive extensive training. They are well-versed in emergency procedures, enabling them to make informed decisions and take effective action in unexpected situations. The emphasis on human oversight and intervention in emergencies is fundamental to safety protocols.

- Environmental Protection Measures. Safety in autonomous shipping extends beyond the ship to the marine environment. Autonomous vessels incorporate measures to minimise environmental impact. These include eco-friendly hull designs, emission control technologies, and strict adherence to ballast water management regulations, preventing the inadvertent spread of invasive species.

- Regular Safety Audits and Inspections. Autonomous ships undergo regular safety audits and inspections to ensure that all safety protocols and fail-safe mechanisms are in optimal working condition. These audits are conducted by independent authorities to uphold the highest safety standards.

- Simulations and Testing. They undergo extensive simulations and testing before autonomous ships embark on maiden voyages. These tests replicate various scenarios, including adverse weather conditions, equipment failures, and navigational challenges. Such rigorous trials ensure that autonomous vessels can handle a myriad of real-world situations with precision and safety.

The safety protocols and fail-safe mechanisms embedded in autonomous shipping are a testament to the industry's commitment to the well-being of those at sea and protecting the marine environment. As these vessels continue to navigate uncharted waters, their dedication to safety and the continuous improvement of safety standards is unwavering, ensuring a future where autonomy is synonymous with maritime security.

PUBLIC PERCEPTION AND ACCEPTANCE

The successful integration of autonomous ships into the maritime landscape hinges on technological prowess and the public's acceptance and understanding of these vessels. As these innovative technologies chart their course on the world's oceans, it is imperative to consider and navigate the complex currents of public perception.

JOB DISPLACEMENT CONCERNS

One of the most significant factors influencing public perception of autonomous shipping is the concern surrounding job displacement within the maritime industry. The public is understandably apprehensive about the potential reduction in seafaring jobs as autonomous vessels promise increased efficiency and reduced labour costs. Addressing these concerns and navigating the transition of maritime professionals to a new era of maritime operations is pivotal for fostering acceptance and understanding.

The transition to autonomous shipping is not about replacing skilled seafarers but transforming their roles. It's essential to emphasise that while some traditional maritime roles may evolve or diminish, new opportunities will emerge. For instance, the operation and management of autonomous vessels require a blend of maritime expertise and technological proficiency. As such, the industry must invest in training and reskilling programs that enable maritime professionals to adapt to and manage these cutting-edge vessels effectively.

Furthermore, the broader maritime ecosystem is expanding, offering vessel monitoring, data analysis, remote diagnostics, cybersecurity, and onshore operations opportunities. Public perception can be positively influenced by highlighting the potential for employment and career growth in these new roles, emphasising that autonomous shipping is not just cutting jobs but evolving careers within the industry.

SAFETY AND SECURITY APPREHENSIONS

Public concerns about autonomous ships' safety and security are well-founded and deserve careful consideration. The public is keenly interested in understanding how these vessels navigate safely, avoid accidents, and manage emergencies. To alleviate these concerns and foster acceptance, it is crucial to prioritise education and transparency regarding safety protocols and fail-safe mechanisms.

First and foremost, safety is a paramount priority in the development and operation of autonomous ships. These vessels are equipped with advanced sensors, artificial intelligence, and precise navigation systems that significantly reduce the risk of human error, a leading cause of maritime accidents. Public education should emphasise that autonomous ships are designed with the latest safety technology and are continually monitored to ensure safe navigation.

Transparency is another key element in addressing public apprehensions. It's essential to provide clear information on how autonomous vessels are equipped to navigate, avoid collisions, and respond swiftly to emergencies. Demonstrating the robust safety measures in place, such as collision avoidance systems, real-time monitoring, and autonomous response mechanisms, can go a long way in assuaging public concerns.

Moreover, involving regulatory authorities, industry stakeholders, and experts in safety certifications ensures that autonomous ships adhere to stringent safety standards. Collaborative efforts and adherence to rigorous safety protocols should be emphasised in public communication to convey the commitment to safety in autonomous shipping.

ENVIRONMENTAL RESPONSIBILITY

Public perception of autonomous shipping is intrinsically tied to the industry's environmental responsibility and sustainability efforts. In a world increasingly committed to environmental stewardship, the extent to which autonomous ships contribute to reducing emissions, protecting marine ecosystems, and minimising ecological impact plays a central role in gaining public acceptance.

To address this concern, it's crucial to highlight the eco-friendly aspects of autonomous ships. Autonomous vessels are designed with sustainability, incorporating advanced technologies that optimise routes and fuel efficiency. These vessels significantly reduce greenhouse gas emissions and the overall environmental footprint of maritime transportation.

Public communication should emphasise the environmental benefits of autonomous shipping, emphasising how these vessels align with global efforts to combat climate change and promote a greener maritime industry. Concrete data and real-world examples of emissions reduction and sustainability practices should be presented to demonstrate the positive impact of autonomous shipping on the planet.

Moreover, engaging with environmental organisations, participating in conservation efforts, and supporting initiatives that protect marine ecosystems can further enhance the industry's reputation for environmental responsibility. Collaboration with such groups can serve as a powerful testament to the commitment to preserving our oceans and the communities that depend on them.

TECHNOLOGY LITERACY

Public acceptance of autonomous shipping is deeply intertwined with technology literacy, and ensuring that the public, particularly those residing in coastal communities, is well-informed about the technology behind autonomous ships is a vital step. Information campaigns and outreach efforts that convey the benefits, safety measures, and ethical considerations of autonomy are crucial for fostering acceptance.

The public's understanding of autonomous ship technology can be enhanced through targeted educational programs, public forums, and informational materials explaining these vessels' principles. Demonstrating meticulous safety measures, such as advanced collision avoidance systems and real-time monitoring, can alleviate apprehensions about the technology.

Additionally, emphasising the ethical considerations surrounding autonomy, such as responsible AI decision-making and adherence to environmental standards, is essential. Public engagement sessions and workshops can facilitate open discussions and address concerns about the ethical implications of autonomous shipping.

Furthermore, involving local communities in developing and implementing autonomous shipping projects can foster a sense of ownership and understanding. By including residents in the decision-making process, their perspectives and concerns can be integrated into the planning and execution of autonomous shipping initiatives.

TRUST IN REGULATORY OVERSIGHT

Public trust in autonomous shipping is significantly influenced by the role of regulatory authorities in ensuring the safety and responsibility of this emerging industry. Establishing comprehensive regulatory frameworks and the unwavering commitment to the highest safety standards play a pivotal role in fostering this trust and promoting public acceptance.

Regulatory authorities, such as the International Maritime Organization (IMO), are tasked with creating harmonised and rigorous standards for autonomous ship operations. These standards encompass safety, navigation, collision avoidance, emergency response, and ethical considerations. Demonstrating the industry's commitment to adhering to these standards is essential for gaining public trust.

To address this concern, it is crucial to communicate transparently about the regulatory frameworks in place and the ongoing efforts to refine and adapt them as technology evolves. Public awareness campaigns can highlight the role of regulatory authorities in overseeing autonomous shipping and ensuring that vessels operate within established maritime rules.

Furthermore, regulatory authorities should actively seek public input and participation in the regulatory process. Public consultations, open forums, and opportunities for feedback can empower the public to have a voice in shaping the regulatory landscape, instilling confidence in the regulatory oversight of autonomous shipping.

ETHICAL QUESTIONS

Ethical questions surrounding autonomous ships, including their decision-making capabilities and accountability in accidents, are subjects of public discourse and significant consideration. Open dialogues that engage the public in addressing these ethical dilemmas and defining the ethical values embedded in autonomous technology are crucial for promoting public acceptance.

Public engagement in ethical discussions can take the form of ethical advisory boards or committees that involve experts, stakeholders, and members of the public in deliberating on the ethical considerations of autonomous shipping. These platforms provide an opportunity to address questions related to AI decision-making, accountability, and the responsible behaviour of autonomous systems.

Furthermore, public education initiatives focusing on autonomous technology's ethical foundations are vital. These initiatives can provide information about the industry's ethical guidelines and principles, ensuring the public is aware of the commitment to ethical decision-making in autonomous ship operations.

Public acceptance can also be enhanced by showcasing examples of ethical practices and responsible AI behaviour in the operation of autonomous vessels. Demonstrating how these ships prioritise ethical considerations and adhere to industry standards can reassure the public.

In summary, building public trust in autonomous shipping involves emphasising the role of regulatory oversight in ensuring safety and adhering to ethical principles. Engaging the public in discussions about ethical questions and the ethical foundations of autonomous technology is a key step in fostering acceptance and understanding of this innovative industry.

EMERGENCY RESPONSE AND HUMAN OVERSIGHT

Public perception of autonomous ships is often more favourable when there is an understanding that human oversight and intervention remain integral to their operation, especially in emergencies. Ensuring that these vessels operate in tandem with skilled crew members or remote operators can instil confidence in the technology and mitigate apprehensions about complete autonomy.

To address this concern, it is essential to emphasise the collaborative nature of autonomous ship operations. Public communication should underscore that while autonomous ships are equipped with advanced AI systems and algorithms for autonomous navigation, they are not devoid of human involvement. Skilled crew members or remote operators are present to monitor vessel operations, intervene when necessary, and make critical decisions in unforeseen situations.

Demonstrating how autonomous ships maintain a safety net of human expertise, especially in emergencies, can alleviate public apprehension. Real-world examples and case studies of successful collaborative responses to emergencies can further reassure the public of the technology's reliability.

SAFETY RECORDS AND INCIDENT RESPONSES

Safety records and how the industry responds to incidents profoundly influence public perception of autonomous shipping. Demonstrating a commitment to safety through incident transparency, thorough investigations, and continuous improvements is crucial in aligning the industry with public expectations.

The industry should prioritise proactive safety measures, emphasising advanced sensors, collision avoidance systems, and robust fail-safe mechanisms. These measures should be communicated to the public as part of a comprehensive safety strategy.

In the event of incidents or accidents, transparency is key. The industry should openly acknowledge such incidents, conduct thorough investigations, and communicate the findings and actions taken to prevent similar incidents. This transparency demonstrates accountability and a commitment to continuous improvement.

Public engagement can further enhance safety records and responses. Involving the public in discussions about safety measures and incident response protocols can help build trust and confidence. Public input and feedback can contribute to refining safety practices and developing new safety standards.

The autonomous shipping industry can align with public expectations and demonstrate its dedication to ensuring safe and responsible operations by prioritising safety and being transparent in safety records and incident responses.

ADVOCACY FOR AUTONOMOUS SHIPPING

Advocacy groups, industry stakeholders, and technology providers are pivotal in championing autonomous shipping. Their efforts to promote autonomy's benefits and address public concerns are essential for widespread acceptance. These groups should engage in comprehensive advocacy efforts to build support for autonomous shipping.

Advocacy initiatives should include educational campaigns that inform the public about the advantages of autonomous shipping, such as enhanced safety, reduced emissions, and cost savings. These campaigns can use various media and communication channels to reach a broad audience.

Engaging in open and constructive dialogues with the public is also crucial. Advocacy groups and industry stakeholders should actively seek feedback and address concerns raised by the public. Transparency and a willingness to respond to questions and doubts can go a long way in building trust.

Additionally, highlighting success stories and real-world applications of autonomous shipping can provide concrete examples of the technology's benefits. Demonstrating the positive impact

71

of autonomy in various sectors, such as cargo transportation and environmental monitoring, can help sway public opinion.

LOCAL ENGAGEMENT AND ECONOMIC IMPACT

Autonomous shipping can have a significant economic impact on coastal communities. Engaging with these communities and communicating the economic opportunities and benefits of autonomous shipping is essential for shaping local perceptions and garnering support.

Local engagement should involve partnerships with community organisations, chambers of commerce, and local government bodies. These collaborations can facilitate discussions about the economic advantages of autonomous shipping, including job creation, increased business activity, and improved infrastructure.

Highlighting case studies and success stories in regions where autonomous shipping has had a positive economic impact can serve as powerful examples. Localised data on job opportunities and revenue generation can provide tangible evidence of the benefits brought to coastal communities.

Furthermore, involving residents in the planning and developing autonomous shipping initiatives can ensure their concerns and interests are considered. Public forums, town hall meetings, and community feedback mechanisms can facilitate this engagement.

Ultimately, advocating for autonomous shipping at the local level and emphasising the positive economic contributions to coastal communities can help generate support and build acceptance within these areas.

Public perception and acceptance represent the linchpin upon which the success of autonomous shipping rests. As these vessels embark on their transformative journey, understanding the dynamics of public sentiment and proactively addressing concerns while fostering awareness and trust is essential to navigating this new era in the maritime industry. Public engagement, open discourse, and a commitment to safety and ethical responsibility are the guiding stars towards ensuring the acceptance of autonomous shipping in society.

Chapter **7**

RESEARCH AND DEVELOPMENT

In the ever-evolving realm of autonomous shipping, pursuing excellence and innovation through research and development is a beacon guiding the industry forward. Chapter Seven explores the vibrant landscape of ongoing research initiatives, the cutting-edge technological advancements in autonomy, and the essential investment in innovation that propels autonomous shipping into uncharted waters.

ONGOING RESEARCH INITIATIVES

Research serves as the foundation upon which the promising future of autonomous shipping is being built. Ongoing research initiatives are pivotal in shaping these innovative vessels, addressing multifaceted challenges that span safety, environmental impact, and technology development. Worldwide, researchers are committed to advancing the frontiers of autonomous shipping in the following key areas.

SAFETY ADVANCEMENTS

The paramount focus of ongoing research initiatives is the continuous refinement of safety measures for autonomous ships. Researchers are dedicated to enhancing the existing safety framework, encompassing areas such as developing more advanced collision avoidance systems. They are working on improving emergency response protocols, ensuring the seamless coordination of autonomous vessels during unforeseen situations. Additionally, research explores the intricate dynamics of human-automation interaction, guaranteeing that the integration of automation leads to a safer maritime environment. This intricate work aims to eliminate potential risks associated with autonomy and fortify the trust in the technology's safety.

ENERGY EFFICIENCY

Researchers are directing their efforts towards optimising energy usage in autonomous vessels. The overarching goal is to enhance the sustainability of maritime transportation. Innovations in propulsion systems are a central focus, with studies aimed at developing more energy-efficient and environmentally responsible systems. Furthermore, research delves into fuel efficiency enhancements, seeking to minimise the environmental footprint of autonomous ships. Researchers are also exploring integrating renewable energy sources in alignment with broader sustainability goals. This includes implementing solar panels and wind propulsion systems to reduce reliance on traditional fossil fuels, contributing to greener and more efficient maritime transportation practices. This ongoing work is a testament to the commitment of researchers to address environmental concerns and shape a more sustainable future for autonomous shipping.

ETHICAL FRAMEWORKS

Ongoing research initiatives in autonomous shipping extend to addressing the intricate ethical considerations associated with the technology. Researchers actively engage in dialogues and investigations to establish robust ethical frameworks that guide the decision-making capabilities of autonomous ships. These frameworks are designed to provide a moral compass for these vessels, ensuring they can navigate complex ethical dilemmas that may arise. Ethical discussions encompass various scenarios, from emergency response decisions to navigation choices in critical situations. By developing ethical guidelines and principles, researchers aim to imbue autonomous ships with responsible and ethical behaviour, instilling trust and confidence in the technology's capacity to make morally sound decisions.

CYBERSECURITY AND DATA PROTECTION

The increasing digitalisation of the maritime industry has made cybersecurity research an imperative component of ongoing initiatives. With the proliferation of connected systems and data-driven operations, safeguarding vessel systems from cyber threats and protecting sensitive data is paramount. Ongoing research efforts are laser-focused on fortifying the cybersecurity measures of autonomous ships. Researchers are dedicated to creating and implementing advanced technologies, protocols, and best practices to ensure the resilience of autonomous vessels against digital intrusions. This work spans data encryption, secure communication protocols, real-time threat detection, and responsive countermeasures. As the digital landscape evolves, researchers remain committed to staying ahead of potential cyber threats, safeguarding the integrity of vessel systems and data, and maintaining the robustness of autonomous ships in the face of digital challenges.

ENVIRONMENTAL MONITORING AND CONSERVATION

Researchers play a crucial role in the ongoing environmental monitoring and conservation efforts in autonomous shipping. These initiatives encompass various studies and technological developments to minimise autonomous vessels' ecological impact and ensure marine environment protection.

One significant aspect of ongoing research involves assessing the ecological impact of autonomous shipping. Researchers conduct extensive studies to understand how these vessels interact with marine ecosystems. This includes examining the effects of autonomous ships on aquatic life, water quality, and the overall health of the ocean environment. Through careful observation and data collection, researchers strive to identify potential risks and opportunities for mitigating environmental adverse effects.

Simultaneously, researchers are committed to developing cutting-edge technologies to safeguard marine life and preserve delicate ecosystems. These efforts encompass the creation of innovative tools and practices for reducing collisions with marine animals, minimising underwater noise pollution, and preventing the release of harmful substances into the ocean.

By engaging in these environmental initiatives, researchers aim to ensure that the rise of autonomous shipping aligns with broader sustainability goals and leads to an efficient, responsible, and environmentally conscious maritime industry. These ongoing efforts reflect a commitment to safeguarding our oceans and preserving the rich biodiversity that thrives within them.

TECHNOLOGICAL ADVANCEMENTS IN AUTONOMY

The heart of autonomous shipping beats with technological advancements redefining what is possible on the open sea. Innovations include navigation systems and artificial intelligence, ensuring that autonomous vessels remain at the forefront of maritime technology.

ADVANCED SENSORS

The evolution of sensor technology is an ongoing journey that equips autonomous ships with a more comprehensive and real-time understanding of their surroundings. Innovations in sensor design and capabilities significantly enhance the vessels' ability to gather an even richer stream of data about their environment. These advanced sensors are the vigilant eyes and ears of autonomous ships, enabling them to detect obstacles, adapt to rapidly changing weather conditions, and refine navigation precision to previously unparalleled levels. Through the continuous evolution of sensor technology, autonomous vessels have developed a heightened situational awareness that empowers them to navigate complex maritime scenarios with enhanced safety and precision.

ARTIFICIAL INTELLIGENCE

In the landscape of autonomous shipping, artificial intelligence (AI) plays a pivotal and continually expanding role. As machine learning algorithms become increasingly sophisticated, AI's contributions to the maritime industry are multifaceted. Beyond the foundational task of aiding in decision-making processes, AI now offers a comprehensive suite of functionalities that revolutionise the operational landscape of autonomous vessels.

One of the standout features of AI in autonomous shipping is its ability to provide predictive maintenance. By analysing vast streams of real-time data generated during voyages, AI can predict and identify technical issues before they escalate into major problems. This predictive maintenance capability ensures that maintenance and repair actions are initiated proactively before a critical system failure occurs. The result is reduced downtime, lower operational disruptions, and enhanced operational efficiency. Shipping companies benefit not only from decreased maintenance expenses but also from more reliable vessel performance.

AI's decision-making capabilities have also evolved significantly. AI algorithms are no longer limited to basic navigation tasks; they can handle complex decision-making scenarios. These systems encompass a range of functions, including route planning, collision avoidance, and adaptation to changing weather conditions. As AI algorithms mature, they empower autonomous ships to operate with a level of autonomy that previously required extensive human intervention. This reduces the need for remote human oversight, making vessels more self-reliant in navigating the complexities of the open sea. It also enhances safety, as these algorithms can make real-time decisions in scenarios that may pose a risk to human crews.

REMOTE OPERATION AND CONTROL

Technological advancements in remote operation and control capabilities are a central driving force behind the progress of autonomous shipping. Over recent years, these advancements have reached a level of precision and sophistication that was once considered unattainable. They are redefining maritime operations, offering unprecedented control and opportunities for increased safety.

Remote operation, in particular, is at the forefront of this progress. Maritime technology now allows for the remote oversight of vessel operations from considerable distances. This shift has significant implications for the industry. Skilled remote operators can effectively manage the intricacies of autonomous vessels, even when they are thousands of miles away from the actual ship. This remote-control level safeguards against potential emergencies or unexpected challenges during voyages. Additionally, it enhances the efficiency of operations by allowing for real-time adjustments and decision-making based on the latest data from the vessel's sensors and systems.

The precision achieved in remote operation and control mechanisms ensures that autonomous ships can adapt effectively to dynamic environments, safely navigate complex maritime scenarios, and respond to unanticipated events. This capacity has positioned autonomous shipping as a revolutionary leap forward in the maritime industry, offering practical advantages and heightened safety measures that once seemed beyond reach. As these technological advancements continue to evolve, they underscore the industry's commitment to shaping a safer, more efficient, and technologically advanced future on the high seas.

COMMUNICATION SYSTEMS

Effective communication systems are the lifeblood of autonomous ships, ensuring seamless connectivity in the complex and often remote maritime environment. These systems represent a cornerstone of the industry's technological advancements, as they address a wide array of critical functions that underpin safety, navigation, and the exchange of essential data.

The advanced communication systems integrated into autonomous ships enable continuous connectivity with a constellation of stakeholders, from other vessels in the vicinity to shoreside operation centres. This constant, real-time communication is vital for ensuring the safety of autonomous ships. It facilitates collision avoidance by sharing navigational data with other vessels, allowing for precise coordination and avoiding potential conflicts. These systems are a key contributor to reducing maritime accidents, one of the primary drivers behind adopting autonomous shipping. Moreover, they enable remote operators and maritime authorities to monitor the status and movements of autonomous vessels, ensuring compliance with navigation rules and responding to emergencies promptly.

Beyond safety, communication systems support various aspects of navigation. They provide vital information on weather conditions, traffic patterns, and navigational hazards, allowing autonomous ships to adjust their routes and actions accordingly. This contributes to the vessels' ability to navigate autonomously and safely, further reducing the need for human intervention. These communication systems are also fundamental for data exchange, supporting the transfer of information that aids in route optimisation, performance analysis, and maintenance planning. In an industry increasingly reliant on data-driven decision-making, these systems form the backbone of the autonomous maritime landscape.

ECO-FRIENDLY PROPULSION

In the quest for sustainability and reduced environmental impact, autonomous ships are at the forefront of innovation in propulsion systems. These technological advancements have paved the way for adopting eco-friendly propulsion technologies that replace traditional fossil fuel engines. The shift towards eco-friendly propulsion signifies a significant step towards a more sustainable and environmentally conscious maritime industry.

Electric propulsion systems are one of the notable eco-friendly alternatives, making their mark in autonomous shipping. These systems utilise electric motors powered by batteries or onboard generators. By substituting traditional internal combustion engines with electric motors, autonomous vessels reduce greenhouse gas emissions, air pollutants, and noise pollution. Electric propulsion systems also offer operational advantages, including lower maintenance requirements, quiet operation, and the capacity to provide precise control over thrust and speed. These innovations contribute to the industry's alignment with global sustainability goals.

Another promising eco-friendly propulsion technology is hydrogen fuel cells. These systems convert hydrogen into electricity to power the ship's electric motors. Hydrogen is considered a clean energy source because water vapour is the only byproduct of its conversion, making it an attractive option for autonomous ships aiming to minimise their ecological impact.

Biofuels, derived from renewable sources like algae or waste materials, are also being explored as an eco-friendly alternative to traditional fossil fuels. These fuels have the potential to significantly reduce greenhouse gas emissions and promote a more sustainable maritime industry.

Adopting these eco-friendly propulsion systems is not only environmentally responsible but also economically advantageous, as they contribute to fuel savings, reduced operational costs, and compliance with stringent emission regulations. As technology continues to evolve, the industry can expect even more innovative and sustainable propulsion solutions that further enhance the environmental profile of autonomous ships.

INVESTMENT IN INNOVATION

In autonomous shipping, innovation thrives on the engine of investment, which propels the industry toward its technological aspirations. Investment in this domain is instrumental in advancing research, fostering development, and turning ambitious visions into tangible realities. Investment in innovation within the autonomous shipping sector encompasses several key dimensions.

First and foremost, industry collaboration stands as a formidable pillar of innovation. Collaboration between technology providers, shipping companies, and research institutions forms the crucible for exchanging ideas and knowledge. These collaborations enable the sharing resources, expertise, and insights, propelling the industry's technological evolution forward. The synergy arising from these collaborations facilitates the acceleration of breakthroughs in autonomy, cementing their place in the future of maritime transport.

Simultaneously, the burgeoning landscape of startups and entrepreneurial endeavours inject creativity into the industry. Investment in these startups gives them essential financial resources and bolsters their ability to pioneer innovative solutions. These dynamic enterprises are unearthing novel ideas and inventive approaches, pushing the boundaries of what autonomous shipping can achieve. Investment here nurtures the seeds of autonomy, allowing them to sprout into groundbreaking technological solutions.

Moreover, the support and commitment of governments and regulatory authorities play a pivotal role. Recognising the significance of autonomous shipping, they actively provide various forms of backing, including financial incentives, funding, and regulatory support. This collective effort significantly contributes to advancing research and development initiatives within the industry. It underpins the development and widespread adoption of autonomous technologies and underscores the importance of autonomous shipping as a transformative force in the maritime world.

Chapter 8

GLOBAL IMPACT

The emergence of autonomous shipping has ushered in a new era in maritime transportation, where the ripple effects extend well beyond the vessels themselves. This chapter ventures into the vast and interconnected domain of global impact, examining the collaborative efforts on an international scale, scrutinising the far-reaching implications on the global shipping market, and navigating the intricate waters of geopolitical considerations.

At the heart of the global impact of autonomous shipping lies international collaboration. Maritime nations increasingly recognise the importance of unified standards and regulations for these innovative vessels. Organisations like the International Maritime Organization (IMO) are at the forefront of these cooperative endeavours, working diligently to create a harmonised regulatory framework that transcends national borders. These efforts are pivotal in ensuring the seamless integration of autonomous ships into global maritime operations. The quest for international collaboration is essential for fostering trust and confidence in these transformative technologies.

The ramifications of autonomous shipping resonate powerfully within the global shipping market. The industry landscape is transforming profoundly as these vessels offer substantial benefits, such as increased safety, operational efficiency, and cost savings. Shipping companies are drawn to autonomy not only for its financial advantages but also for the competitive edge it bestows. Early adopters find themselves ahead of the curve, reducing costs and enhancing their offerings, influencing the broader market. Furthermore, the shift towards autonomous shipping opens doors for diversified vessel types, from cargo carriers to research vessels and offshore platforms, expanding the spectrum of maritime applications. In response to these shifts, the market is recalibrating its dynamics, with established maritime service providers diversifying their offerings to encompass autonomous ship management services.

However, amid these tides of transformation, geopolitical considerations emerge as a critical facet of the global impact. Autonomous shipping adoption is subject to geopolitical factors, including territorial claims, international agreements, and economic interests. The newfound capabilities of these vessels to operate in remote and hazardous environments, such as the Arctic's ice-covered waters or offshore oil platforms, raise questions about sovereignty, jurisdiction, and resource exploitation. Geopolitical dynamics come to the forefront as nations navigate how to harness the potential of autonomous shipping within the bounds of international law and diplomacy.

In this chapter, we set sail on a journey across the global seas of autonomous shipping's impact, from the cooperative currents of international collaboration to the market's shifting tides and the geopolitical crosswinds that shape this innovative era of maritime transportation.

INTERNATIONAL COLLABORATION ON AUTONOMOUS SHIPPING

The world of autonomous shipping thrives on collaboration across borders. Nations and organisations are joining to create a collective foundation for this transformative technology.

INTERNATIONAL REGULATORY FRAMEWORKS

The journey towards embracing autonomous shipping is not taken lightly in the maritime world. It is a voyage through uncharted waters where the game's rules are being rewritten to accommodate this transformative technology. At the forefront of this evolution are the ongoing efforts to establish international regulatory frameworks that will serve as the guiding lights for autonomous shipping on a global scale.

The complexity of the maritime landscape, with its interplay of international waters, territorial sovereignty, and a myriad of vessel types, presents a unique set of challenges. As such, it's no surprise that international collaboration has emerged as the foundational principle in shaping these regulatory frameworks. Maritime nations are coming together in a concerted effort to define unified standards that ensure the safe and responsible operation of autonomous vessels. Organisational powerhouses such as the International Maritime Organization (IMO) lead this endeavour, orchestrating dialogues and negotiations that bridge international boundaries.

These collaborative endeavours serve several critical purposes. First and foremost, they work to foster trust and confidence in the technology by establishing clear-cut guidelines that govern the use of autonomous vessels. Safety and environmental considerations, navigation rules, and emergency procedures are among the many aspects that these frameworks aim to standardise. Harmonising these standards across borders ensures that autonomous ships can navigate the world's oceans seamlessly without encountering inconsistent regulations at every turn.

Furthermore, establishing international regulatory frameworks responds to the need for clarity. This is critical in an industry where questions of liability, insurance, and accident investigations can be complex and multifaceted. The regulatory frameworks serve as a beacon, offering guidance and predictability to all stakeholders involved in autonomous shipping, from ship operators to technology providers and regulatory authorities.

Moreover, they provide a roadmap for nations navigating the legal, diplomatic, and economic implications of autonomous shipping. The collaborative efforts reflect a broader acknowledgement of the need to come to terms with this paradigm shift in maritime transportation. Nations adapt to an era where their territorial waters and economic interests can be influenced by vessels that operate with greater autonomy and precision.

In the grand narrative of autonomous shipping, international regulatory frameworks are the sturdy anchors that keep the industry grounded and ensure its responsible and safe evolution. As nations steer their vessels through these uncharted waters, establishing these frameworks is an essential lighthouse that guides the way, offering assurance to the maritime world that autonomous shipping is here to stay and will sail under international cooperation and compliance.

INFORMATION SHARING AND RESEARCH

The age-old saying that "knowledge is power" takes on new meaning in autonomous shipping. In the journey towards harnessing the full potential of autonomous vessels, nations understand the profound importance of information sharing and collaborative research initiatives.

Across the global maritime community, the challenges posed by autonomous shipping are not unique to a single nation's waters. They transcend borders and territorial seas, making the oceans a shared domain. As a result, nations recognise that their journeys towards adopting autonomous shipping can be expedited through cooperation, knowledge exchange, and collaborative research endeavours.

One of the paramount factors driving this international collaboration is the shared nature of the challenges involved in autonomous shipping. From safety and security concerns to the intricacies of navigating international waters, a common thread binds nations in their quest for understanding and mastery of this technology. The implications of autonomous shipping stretch far beyond economic considerations. They touch upon safety, ethics, the environment, and geopolitics questions.

As a result, information sharing has become a vital currency among maritime nations. The experiences, insights, and lessons learned by one nation can hold immense value for another. This knowledge exchange occurs through diplomatic channels, conferences, research initiatives, and industry forums. Such forums provide a space for discussions that shape the course of autonomous shipping on a global scale.

Collaborative research initiatives are another cornerstone of this cooperation. Researchers from different nations join hands to explore the multifaceted aspects of autonomous shipping. Whether refining safety measures, exploring the environmental impact, or studying the ethical and legal implications of autonomy, these initiatives draw from a wealth of global expertise. The pooling of resources and shared objectives expedite progress, helping all maritime nations stay on the cutting edge of autonomous technology.

These collaborative efforts go beyond the technological dimension of autonomy and contribute to a shared understanding of the fundamental tenets and principles that will govern the maritime industry's future. This shared understanding is critical in establishing consistent standards and regulatory frameworks that will serve as the guiding light for autonomous shipping on an international scale.

In the grand tapestry of autonomous shipping, the threads of cooperation and collaboration spun by maritime nations form a resilient and interconnected network. It's a network that defies the boundaries of territorial waters and sovereignty, recognising that the oceans are a shared realm. Information sharing and collaborative research are the lighthouses that guide nations through these uncharted waters, providing them with a collective vision and understanding of the technology's potential and its responsible integration into the global maritime community.

KNOWLEDGE EXCHANGE

The pursuit of autonomous shipping represents an uncharted journey into a world of technological innovation. This quest for autonomy transcends national borders, making it essential for institutions, universities, research organisations, and technology providers to engage in international knowledge exchange programs. This knowledge exchange is a linchpin in the swift evolution of autonomous technologies, fuelling their development and responsible implementation.

At the heart of this global exchange is a commitment to the free flow of expertise, experiences, and the latest advancements in autonomy. Universities and research institutions, as the vanguards of cutting-edge research, are instrumental in fostering this transnational knowledge sharing. Their role extends beyond technology development to the dissemination of knowledge across boundaries. Through collaborative research projects, joint initiatives, and academic partnerships, institutions facilitate the exchange of insights from the latest breakthroughs.

International knowledge exchange programs are not limited to academia alone. Technology providers play a pivotal role in this network with their deep expertise in autonomy. They are innovation hubs and actively engage in initiatives to share best practices and technological developments. Their expertise extends to onboard systems, communication technologies, and navigational advancements integral to autonomous vessels' operation. This partnership between technology providers and research institutions forms a collaborative ecosystem where the power of shared knowledge is magnified.

This knowledge transfer across borders is a catalyst for accelerating autonomous technologies. Nations can learn from each other's successes and challenges, avoiding the redundancy of reinventing the wheel. Instead, they can build upon the collective experience of others, adapting their strategies for the rapid development and deployment of autonomous vessels.

MULTINATIONAL ALLIANCES

The concept of autonomous shipping transcends territorial waters, and the oceans form a shared domain for all maritime nations. This shared space demands a harmonisation of regulations and standards. Multinational alliances have emerged between nations and industry stakeholders, a testament to cooperation and understanding. These alliances are driven by the vision of establishing a consistent and universally accepted framework for autonomous shipping.

These partnerships recognise the impracticality of isolating regulatory efforts to national boundaries. The essence of the oceans as a shared realm requires mutual recognition of safety protocols and common standards. Multinational alliances aim to facilitate the deployment of autonomous vessels in international waters with the assurance of consistent regulations that protect the technology and the marine environment.

These alliances foster diplomatic dialogues and engagements that harmonise regulations by bringing together nations and industry players. The collaborative efforts bridge gaps between regions and regulatory bodies, ensuring that a mosaic of conflicting standards does not stifle the technology.

Furthermore, these alliances serve to address the complexities of liability and responsibility. As autonomous shipping introduces new dimensions to the traditional maritime landscape, questions of accountability require international cooperation. Multinational alliances create a platform for discussions on liability mechanisms and mechanisms for risk-sharing in the autonomous era.

In the grand maritime narrative, knowledge exchange and multinational alliances are the threads that connect nations and industry stakeholders across the world. They bridge the rough waters of technological innovation, enabling nations to share insights, pool expertise, and collectively navigate the autonomous horizon. These networks are instrumental in ensuring that the potential of autonomous shipping is harnessed responsibly and universally accepted, making the world's oceans a safer, more efficient, and interconnected arena for maritime operations.

GLOBAL SHIPPING MARKET IMPLICATIONS

The adoption of autonomous shipping reverberates throughout the global shipping market, ushering in a wave of transformative implications.

1. ENHANCED EFFICIENCY AND COST SAVINGS

Autonomous shipping represents a significant leap forward in maritime transportation, and at its core, it's an efficiency-driven revolution. One of the most compelling aspects of autonomy is its ability to optimise practically every facet of ship operations. By integrating advanced sensors, AI-driven algorithms, and real-time data analysis, autonomous vessels achieve unparalleled efficiency, all while charting the most efficient routes across the world's oceans.

These optimised routes are not merely convenient; they have far-reaching economic implications. For shipping companies, the ability to identify the shortest, fastest, and most fuel-efficient routes is a game-changer. The direct impact is a substantial reduction in fuel consumption and operational costs. This reduction in fuel consumption, combined with the optimisation of speed and cargo distribution, results in significant cost savings. Autonomous ships can precisely navigate turbulent waters and adverse weather conditions, ensuring fuel is expended judiciously.

This heightened efficiency translates into more economical international trade, a cornerstone of the global economy. Shipping companies can provide their clients with more cost-effective transport solutions, contributing to a competitive and interconnected world marketplace. Reduced shipping costs have a cascading effect on various industries that depend on maritime transportation, including the shipping of consumer goods, raw materials, and energy resources. The economic implications ripple across the supply chain, benefiting consumers through lower prices and businesses through increased cost-efficiency.

2. LABOR MARKET DISRUPTION

The advent of autonomous shipping introduces a wave of transformation in the maritime labour market. The traditional seafaring roles, deeply rooted in the history of maritime trade, face disruption as autonomous vessels require fewer crew members. This shift raises pivotal questions surrounding job displacement and the retraining of maritime professionals.

As the maritime industry adopts greater levels of autonomy, the direct impact on crew requirements becomes apparent. Crew members aboard autonomous vessels have distinct roles that differ from traditional mariners, focusing on monitoring, system management, and intervention during emergencies. While reducing crew size is an operational efficiency, it also challenges the seafaring workforce.

Job displacement concerns emerge as traditional roles aboard ships become less relevant. Maritime professionals who have built their careers on sailing the high seas must adapt to this new reality. The task ahead is twofold: maritime workers must identify new career paths within the evolving maritime ecosystem, and the industry must support their retraining and transition.

The shift towards remote monitoring and control centres is a promising avenue for workforce adaptation. Maritime professionals can find new opportunities as autonomous vessel operators, overseeing ship operations from onshore locations. However, these positions require technological proficiency and a deep understanding of autonomous systems.

Therefore, addressing the labour market disruption necessitates a concerted effort between the maritime industry, educational institutions, and governments. Educational and training programs that prepare maritime workers for autonomous shipping roles are essential. Providing support for their transition is a matter of ensuring a skilled workforce and a reflection of the industry's commitment to the well-being of its professionals.

The impact of autonomous shipping on the labour market is not merely a challenge but an opportunity for reskilling and career advancement. The evolving nature of the industry demands the engagement of maritime professionals in lifelong learning and the acquisition of new technological skills, setting the course for a brighter future in the autonomous maritime era.

3. ENVIRONMENTAL SUSTAINABILITY

In its march towards a more sustainable future, the global maritime community finds a compelling ally in autonomous shipping. The industry's steadfast commitment to environmental sustainability is the key to this partnership. Autonomous vessels are innovative marvels and torchbearers for eco-conscious practices, significantly contributing to preserving our planet's delicate ecosystem.

The journey towards environmental sustainability begins with the intrinsic capabilities of autonomous ships. Through advanced route optimisation and fuel efficiency, these vessels seamlessly align with the broader sustainability goals of the maritime industry. The deployment of autonomous ships promises a substantial reduction in greenhouse gas emissions. By continuously assessing environmental conditions, such as weather patterns and ocean currents, autonomous vessels chart routes that optimise fuel consumption and minimise their carbon footprint.

In addition to optimising routes, the very design of autonomous ships incorporates eco-friendly practices. Innovative hull designs are tailored to reduce hydrodynamic resistance. By expending less energy to move through the water, these vessels achieve a double victory – they consume less fuel and thus produce fewer emissions. The maritime industry's carbon footprint is thus diminished, making a profound impact in the fight against climate change.

However, environmental sustainability doesn't end with emissions reduction. The sea, with its fragile marine ecosystems, demands our stewardship. Autonomous ships with sophisticated sensors support marine life protection and environmental monitoring efforts. They collect invaluable data on ocean conditions, aiding in scientific research, oceanography, and marine biology. By enhancing our understanding of the marine environment, autonomous vessels play an active role in conservation, and this contribution is integral to the maritime industry's commitment to protecting marine ecosystems.

4. ECONOMIC GROWTH IN COASTAL COMMUNITIES

The impact of autonomous shipping isn't confined to the vast expanse of the open sea; it extends its influence to the shores of coastal communities. As autonomous vessels come to life, they set in motion a series of economic ripples that breathe new life into these regions. The dawn of autonomy results in more than just the ships themselves; it catalyses the creation of advanced infrastructure, support services, and various technology-related jobs.

Coastal communities thrive in this autonomous era. The adoption of autonomous shipping encourages economic growth through the establishment of advanced infrastructure that supports these vessels. Ports and harbours embrace automation, deploying state-of-the-art cargo-handling equipment and pilotless tugboats, streamlining logistics and improving overall port efficiency. This modernisation of ports leads to increased cargo throughput and smoother operations, rendering these communities integral to global trade and transportation networks.

The potential of autonomous shipping spawns an entire ecosystem of support services. Companies specialising in vessel monitoring, maintenance, and technology-related services spring to life, creating a web of economic activities around these autonomous ships. The digital backbone of autonomous shipping, comprising communication systems, remote monitoring facilities, and diagnostic services, provides fertile ground for technology-related job opportunities. Autonomous ships don't just sail the seas; they drive technology advancements, fostering a robust maritime tech sector.

This era of autonomous shipping isn't just a revolution on the water; it's a catalyst for coastal communities to reimagine their economic landscape. These regions become hubs of innovation, hubs of opportunity, and engines of prosperity, all thanks to the economic growth fuelled by the vessels that autonomously navigate the world's oceans.

5. MARKET COMPETITIVENESS

In the ever-shifting global trade landscape, staying competitive is a paramount objective for shipping companies. The emergence of autonomous shipping heralds an era where competitiveness takes on a new dimension. With their promise of faster transit times, enhanced reliability, and operational efficiency, autonomous vessels have emerged as the harbinger of success and differentiation in the global shipping market.

The introduction of autonomous shipping technology introduces a significant paradigm shift in the world of logistics. These vessels, equipped with advanced AI-driven algorithms, offer optimised routes and speed management. This translates into reduced voyage durations, leading to faster cargo delivery. The impact is felt not only by the shipping companies themselves but also by the broader supply chain. Reduced delivery times mean quicker access to goods for customers and businesses. The just-in-time delivery model becomes more than a concept; it becomes a reality.

Faster transit times are not the only arrow in the quiver of autonomous vessels. These ships come with an inherent advantage of enhanced reliability. The reliability of autonomous systems, combined with state-of-the-art sensors and AI, contributes to risk reduction. One significant contributor to maritime accidents is minimised with reduced human intervention, ensuring smoother, safer, and more reliable voyages. This reliability is a gold standard in a competitive market.

Adopting autonomous technology yields more than a competitive edge; it is the gateway to operational efficiency. The AI-driven algorithms optimise speed and propulsion systems, ensuring minimal energy consumption and maximum operational efficiency. Fuel savings become substantial, and this is reflected in operational costs. Shipping companies leveraging the efficiency of autonomous vessels benefit from cost savings and enhanced profitability. They are poised to offer their clients more reliable, more efficient cargo transport solutions.

Competition in the global shipping market is not just a battle for market share; it's a race towards sustainability and technological prowess. The companies that adopt autonomous shipping lead the charge in technology and sustainability. They align with environmental goals by reducing emissions and the environmental footprint of the maritime industry. This commitment to sustainability is not just a competitive advantage; it's a badge of honour in an industry that recognises the importance of eco-conscious practices.

In this landscape, competitiveness is no longer just about pricing and logistics. It's about adopting innovation, delivering superior services, and embracing a sustainable future. Shipping companies that incorporate autonomous vessels into their fleets are not just competing for business; they are shaping the future of global trade. They are the pioneers of an autonomous era that offers faster, more reliable, and more sustainable maritime transportation solutions. In this era, competitiveness is the engine of progress, the vehicle for transformation, and the lighthouse guiding the global shipping industry into the future.

GEOPOLITICAL CONSIDERATIONS

As autonomous shipping continues to advance and reshape the maritime industry, it inevitably introduces a host of geopolitical considerations that ripple across the world stage. These geopolitical dynamics are poised to have a far-reaching impact on various aspects of international relations, trade, and security.

1. MARITIME SECURITY

Introducing autonomous vessels to the maritime landscape represents a significant shift in maritime security. It raises concerns and considerations that extend beyond conventional maritime defence. As autonomous shipping routes become more prevalent, nations find themselves at the intersection of technology, security, and global trade. Addressing these security implications is paramount to safeguarding the stability and integrity of the world's oceans.

Nations must adapt their maritime security strategies to accommodate the unique characteristics of autonomous vessels. The vulnerabilities these ships might face, such as cyber threats or the potential for uncrewed ships to be used in piracy or terrorism, necessitate a comprehensive re-evaluation of security measures. This includes developing advanced cybersecurity protocols to protect onboard systems, ensuring that autonomous vessels comply with international security standards, and enhancing surveillance and monitoring capabilities to swiftly detect and respond to security threats.

Additionally, international cooperation is vital in addressing these maritime security concerns. Nations must collaborate to establish standardised security protocols and share intelligence related to autonomous shipping. This collective approach ensures that security challenges are met with a unified front and that the vulnerabilities of autonomous vessels are effectively mitigated. In a world where maritime security is a shared responsibility, the safety and protection of autonomous shipping routes become a global imperative.

2. STRATEGIC AUTONOMY

Adopting autonomous shipping technologies carries significant geopolitical implications for nations striving to attain strategic autonomy in maritime transportation. Strategic autonomy is the pursuit of self-sufficiency in transportation and logistics, reducing reliance on external sources for goods and ensuring the uninterrupted flow of essential commodities.

Autonomous shipping plays a pivotal role in this quest for strategic autonomy, offering the potential for nations to gain more control over their supply chains and transportation networks. By integrating autonomous vessels into their logistics systems, countries can secure reliable and efficient transportation channels for goods and resources. This reduces their dependency on external carriers and minimises their vulnerability to disruptions caused by geopolitical conflicts, natural disasters, or other unforeseen events.

To achieve strategic autonomy, nations must invest in developing and deploying autonomous vessels, build the necessary infrastructure, and create favourable regulatory frameworks supporting these technologies. They must also engage in domestic and international strategic partnerships to secure the necessary resources and expertise. Pursuing strategic autonomy through autonomous shipping represents a geopolitical strategy to enhance a nation's resilience, competitiveness, and security in an interconnected world.

3. INTERNATIONAL RELATIONS

The deployment of autonomous vessels catalyses strengthened international relations, fostering collaboration among nations in defining global standards and ensuring the security of shared maritime domains. As autonomous shipping becomes a pervasive sea force, geopolitical considerations are increasingly characterised by cooperative autonomy, trade, and security efforts.

Nations recognise the interdependence that comes with the widespread adoption of autonomous vessels. Collaborative initiatives are underway to establish international regulations and standards that govern the operation of these vessels, ensuring a harmonised approach to safety, navigation, and environmental protection. Shared interests in the success of autonomous shipping drive diplomatic engagements, leading to the creation of frameworks that facilitate cross-border cooperation and information exchange.

Trade agreements and partnerships are also evolving to accommodate the transformative impact of autonomous shipping. Nations are negotiating and adapting trade policies to integrate the benefits of efficient and cost-effective autonomous logistics. This collaborative approach facilitates the global adoption of autonomous vessels and fosters a sense of shared responsibility in navigating the challenges and opportunities presented by this technological evolution.

4. SOVEREIGNTY AND JURISDICTION

The operation of autonomous vessels in international waters raises complex questions about sovereignty and jurisdiction that require careful consideration on the global stage. Nations grapple with the challenge of asserting their authority over these vessels while ensuring the smooth and secure functioning of autonomous shipping across borders.

By their nature, autonomous vessels traverse vast expanses of international waters, complicating traditional notions of maritime sovereignty. Nations are engaging in diplomatic dialogues and negotiations to establish protocols that define the rights and responsibilities of states regarding the operation, regulation, and control of autonomous vessels. Key considerations include jurisdictional boundaries, flag state responsibilities, and mechanisms for resolving disputes that may arise in the autonomous shipping realm.

Cooperative agreements and international conventions become essential tools for addressing these complex issues. Establishing a clear framework that respects the sovereignty of individual nations while promoting the effective governance of autonomous shipping on a global scale is crucial for navigating the evolving geopolitical landscape. As nations navigate these waters together, the balance between asserting sovereignty and fostering international cooperation remains at the forefront of discussions surrounding the future of autonomous vessels.

CASE STUDIES

The journey of autonomous shipping is an unfolding narrative marked by real-world experiences that paint a vivid picture of success, challenges, and the invaluable lessons learned along the way. This chapter presents a comprehensive collection of illuminating case studies that exemplify the remarkable triumphs, the formidable hurdles faced, and the wealth of wisdom derived from the practical deployment of autonomous vessels. These cases not only shed light on the transformative impact of autonomy in diverse maritime sectors but also provide valuable insights into the future of this groundbreaking industry.

SUCCESSFUL IMPLEMENTATIONS OF AUTONOMOUS SHIPS

1. THE YARA BIRKELAND

The Yara Birkeland, a pioneering autonomous container ship, embarked on its maiden voyage in Norwegian waters. Developed as a collaboration between Yara International and technology partners, this vessel is designed to transport fertiliser between three ports in Norway. It signifies a significant step forward in applying autonomy in cargo transport, showcasing the potential for enhanced efficiency, reduced operational costs, and decreased emissions in maritime shipping.

2. THE MAYFLOWER AUTONOMOUS SHIP

The Mayflower Autonomous Ship project, named in homage to its historic predecessor, made headlines with its ambitious transatlantic journey. This autonomous vessel leveraged cutting-edge technology, including advanced sensors, artificial intelligence, and remote-control capabilities, to navigate the Atlantic Ocean autonomously. The project demonstrated the potential for autonomous ships in long-distance marine exploration and research, showcasing advancements in autonomy and remote operation.

3. THE RIO TINTO AUTONOMOUS IRON ORE TRAINS

Although not ships, the Rio Tinto autonomous iron ore trains in Western Australia exemplify the success of autonomous technology in the broader transport sector. These fully autonomous trains transport iron ore from mines to ports, covering vast distances. They operate without onboard crew members and have proven efficient and safe, underscoring the potential of autonomy in various transportation modes.

4. THE BJØRG PAULINE

The Bjørg Pauline is an autonomous offshore vessel that has been deployed in the field of marine aquaculture. Equipped with advanced sensor systems and autonomous operation capabilities, this vessel monitors fish farm conditions, administers feed, and contributes to sustainable and environmentally responsible aquaculture practices. The success of the Bjørg

Pauline demonstrates the versatility of autonomous vessels in various marine applications beyond traditional shipping.

These successful implementations highlight the versatility and promise of autonomous ships in different maritime industry sectors. They show how technology, innovation, and collaboration transform vessels, emphasising safety, efficiency, and environmental responsibility.

REAL-WORLD CHALLENGES FACED AND SOLUTIONS

The implementation of autonomous ships has been challenging. This section presents real-world challenges and the innovative solutions devised to overcome them.

1. REGULATORY COMPLIANCE

Achieving regulatory compliance in the evolving world of autonomous shipping was a multifaceted challenge. As the industry embraced cutting-edge technology, traditional maritime regulations needed to adapt to the autonomous era. This required extensive collaboration among industry stakeholders, including shipping companies, technology providers, and regulatory authorities. The shared goal was to establish unified standards and guidelines to ensure compliance and the global safe and responsible operation of autonomous vessels. This cooperative effort resulted in a regulatory framework that accounts for the unique aspects of autonomy, such as human-automation interaction, safety protocols, and emergency procedures. It is a testament to the industry's commitment to upholding the highest standards while pioneering transformative technology.

2. CYBERSECURITY THREATS

The digitalisation of the maritime industry brought forth a new set of challenges, including cybersecurity threats to autonomous vessels. As these ships rely on complex digital systems and connectivity for navigation, communication, and data exchange, they became potential cyberattack targets. The industry responded proactively, recognising the critical importance of safeguarding onboard systems and sensitive data. Robust cybersecurity measures, including advanced encryption, intrusion detection systems, and continuous monitoring, were implemented to protect autonomous ships against digital intrusions. A culture of constant vigilance was fostered, ensuring that cybersecurity remained a top priority. The industry's resilience in these emerging threats exemplifies its dedication to autonomous vessels' safe and secure operation.

3. CREW TRANSITION

The transition from traditional crewed vessels to autonomous ones marked a significant milestone in the autonomous shipping journey. It brought about a pivotal challenge - addressing concerns about job displacement and ensuring a smooth transition for maritime professionals. The industry recognised the need to embrace innovative solutions, going beyond the deployment of autonomous technology to consider the human element. In response, comprehensive training programs and support services were developed. These programs not only equipped seafarers with the skills necessary to adapt to the new era of autonomous shipping but also opened doors to exciting career opportunities within the autonomous vessel operation and management sector. This thoughtful approach to crew transition was a testament to the industry's commitment to supporting its workforce through transformative changes.

4. HUMAN-AUTOMATION INTERACTION

The success of autonomous shipping depended on creating a seamless and efficient interaction between humans and automation. Navigating the intricate waters of human-automation interaction presented its own set of challenges. To address this, the industry invested in extensive research and development efforts. The result was the development of autonomous vessels with intuitive control interfaces that offered a user-friendly experience. These interfaces empowered crew members and remote operators to effectively manage and monitor vessel operations. The ability to strike a harmonious balance between human expertise and automation prowess was instrumental in the industry's journey towards autonomous shipping, showcasing a commitment to ensuring that technology serves as an ally, not a barrier.

LESSONS LEARNED

The case studies in this chapter offer a treasure trove of lessons learned, providing invaluable insights into the journey of autonomous shipping.

1. COLLABORATION IS KEY

The successful implementation of autonomous shipping hinges on a collaborative approach involving industry stakeholders and governments. Collaboration is the cornerstone of a smooth transition to autonomy. Unified standards and regulations create a clear path towards widespread acceptance and ensure common rules governing autonomous vessels' operation. Through this collaborative effort, the autonomous shipping industry can thrive, fostering trust and consistency on a global scale.

2. SAFETY IS PARAMOUNT

While the journey to autonomous shipping is marked by innovation and technological advancement, safety remains the bedrock upon which the industry is built. Safety isn't just a priority; it's a fundamental requirement. Autonomous vessels must be equipped with rigorous safety protocols, redundancy systems, and fail-safe mechanisms to mitigate risks and ensure the well-being of the vessel, its cargo, and the environment. The commitment to safety is non-negotiable, and this unwavering dedication instils confidence in the industry's ability to deliver on the promise of autonomous shipping while ensuring security and peace of mind on the open seas.

3. CONTINUOUS INNOVATION

The case studies presented in this chapter underscore a fundamental principle of autonomous shipping. They serve as a reminder that the journey of autonomy is ever-evolving, where adaptation and technological refinement are imperative. Success in autonomous shipping is contingent on the industry's ability to adapt to changing circumstances, refine existing technologies, and stay at the forefront of maritime innovation. The case studies reflect the dynamic nature of autonomous shipping, emphasising the need for ongoing research and development. This relentless pursuit of improvement ensures the long-term success and sustainability of autonomous vessels in the maritime landscape.

4. PUBLIC AWARENESS

The case studies also illuminate the significance of public awareness and understanding. While the industry advances technologically, keeping the public well-informed about the benefits, safety measures, and ethical considerations associated with autonomous shipping is essential. Education and outreach efforts are pivotal in garnering support and fostering acceptance. As autonomous vessels become a more prominent part of the maritime world, maintaining open and transparent communication with the public is central to their successful integration. Through these initiatives, autonomous shipping can navigate the complex currents of public perception and secure its place on the world's oceans.

Chapter Nine captures the essence of autonomous shipping through real-world cases of triumph, challenges, and the wisdom gained in the journey. These cases are not merely stories but living proofs of the transformative power of technology, the resilience of the industry, and the remarkable spirit of innovation propelling maritime autonomy into a new era.

FUTURE CHALLENGES AND UNCERTAINTIES

The voyage of autonomous shipping has been characterised by innovation, promise, and transformative change. As we steer into Chapter Ten, the horizon presents a mixture of challenges and uncertainties that lie ahead in the uncharted waters of autonomy. The chapter ahead explores the untrodden path, from unforeseen technological hurdles that may surface as the industry advances to the dynamic shifts in the maritime market that may introduce both opportunities and complexities. We also chart the course through the transformative effects of societal and regulatory shifts that are set to reshape the future of autonomous shipping.

This chapter acknowledges that the journey into autonomy is not devoid of obstacles. We set our sights on the unforeseen technological challenges that may arise, reminding us that adaptability and innovation must be our guiding stars in overcoming these hurdles. The complexities of autonomous navigation, system failures, and ever-evolving technology integration demand constant vigilance and the readiness to navigate uncharted territory.

As we navigate the waters of evolving market dynamics, we anticipate increased competition, economic disparities, and the need for extensive infrastructure development. The maritime market's evolving dynamics bring opportunities and challenges that call for resilience and adaptability within the industry and among coastal communities.

Societal and regulatory shifts are the winds that will shape the sails of autonomous shipping. Public acceptance, workforce transition, ethical considerations, and the ongoing adaptation of regulations are the societal and regulatory challenges that mark the journey. Navigating these shifting currents will be vital to the industry's success as these issues transform.

Chapter Ten is a reminder that the journey into autonomy is dynamic and evolving. It is a testament to the industry's resilience, innovation, and adaptability. It is an invitation to steer with a steady hand and a forward-looking spirit as we navigate the future challenges and uncertainties that come with the promise of a safer, more efficient, and environmentally responsible maritime future.

UNFORESEEN TECHNOLOGICAL HURDLES

A spirit of innovation and discovery marks technological progress in autonomous shipping, but it is not without its unexpected challenges. As the industry advances, unforeseen technological hurdles may emerge to test the resilience and adaptability of autonomous systems. These hurdles can take various forms, including system failures, navigational complexities, edge cases that challenge decision-making algorithms, and the integration of new and evolving technologies.

System failures, for instance, can pose sudden challenges in the operation of autonomous vessels, requiring rapid and efficient responses to ensure the safety of maritime operations.

Navigational complexities might arise in unusual traffic patterns, adverse weather conditions, or unpredictable obstacles in busy ports, demanding that autonomous systems adapt effectively to these dynamic scenarios. Edge cases, or exceptional scenarios beyond typical operating conditions, may reveal new challenges in autonomous decision-making, requiring the industry to be prepared for a broad spectrum of unforeseen situations.

Integrating emerging technologies and their seamless incorporation into autonomous systems is another hurdle, demanding constant adaptation and improvement. As the industry charts its course through uncharted technological waters, these unforeseen challenges will be met with innovation and resilience, forging a path toward greater autonomy in maritime operations.

EVOLVING MARKET DYNAMICS

The adoption of autonomous shipping brings with it a shift in the dynamics of the maritime market, introducing both opportunities and challenges that demand the industry's full attention. One of the prominent dynamics is the intensified market competition. As more companies embrace autonomous vessels, the landscape becomes increasingly competitive, emphasising the need for efficiency, reliability, and cost-effectiveness to maintain a competitive edge.

This shift also touches on economic disparities, as the economic impact of autonomous shipping may not be uniformly distributed across regions. While autonomy can bring economic prosperity to coastal communities, it also raises questions about addressing social and economic inequalities. The transition to autonomy involves extensive infrastructure development, encompassing autonomous ports, navigation systems, and supportive infrastructure, further emphasising the complexity of these market dynamics. Insurance and liability, a fundamental aspect of maritime operations, must adapt to the unique challenges of autonomous shipping, where determining liability in the event of accidents or malfunctions presents a novel set of complexities.

In this evolving market, navigating these shifting dynamics while promoting efficiency, sustainability, and economic fairness becomes paramount for the industry and the coastal regions it affects.

SOCIETAL AND REGULATORY SHIFTS

The future of autonomous shipping is intertwined with profound societal and regulatory changes set to reshape the maritime landscape. Among these transformative forces, public acceptance and understanding are central considerations. As autonomous vessels become a more common sight on the seas, the public's perceptions are continually evolving. Ensuring that the public comprehends the benefits, safety measures, and ethical considerations of autonomous shipping is vital. Industry efforts to educate and engage with the public play a pivotal role in shaping public sentiment and building trust in this technology.

Workforce transition is another societal shift that the industry must address. The transition from traditional, crewed vessels to autonomous ones raises questions about job displacement and the retraining of maritime professionals. Innovative training programs and support services are essential for facilitating this transition and providing seafarers with new career opportunities within the maritime sector.

Ethical considerations are at the forefront of societal change in autonomous shipping. The industry is actively developing ethical frameworks that guide the decision-making capabilities of autonomous vessels, addressing complex ethical dilemmas that may arise in the future. These frameworks aim to ensure that autonomy aligns with societal values, promoting responsible and ethical decisions in a variety of scenarios.

Developing comprehensive frameworks for autonomous shipping remains a significant challenge on the regulatory front. The industry must collaborate with governments and international bodies to establish unified standards that ensure the safe and responsible operation of autonomous vessels. This ongoing adaptation of regulations is essential for harmonising international standards and addressing the complexities of autonomous operations across borders.

The era of autonomous shipping is not just a technological shift but a transformative force that impacts society, the workforce, and the legal landscape. Navigating these shifts requires technical expertise, a deep understanding of public sentiment, a commitment to ethical practices, and a harmonised approach to regulations. As autonomous shipping continues its journey, these societal and regulatory changes are integral components that will shape its path and redefine the maritime industry.

SUMMARY

Chapter Ten has provided a comprehensive exploration of the future challenges and uncertainties that autonomous shipping faces as it charts a course into uncharted waters. This final chapter of our journey reflects the ever-evolving nature of autonomy in maritime operations, marked by a blend of promise and obstacles.

Unforeseen technological hurdles are a reminder that innovation is a dynamic process. The chapter has highlighted that system failures, complex navigational scenarios, edge cases that challenge autonomous decision-making, and integrating new technologies may pose challenges that require innovative solutions. These unforeseen technological hurdles serve as a call to be ever-vigilant and adaptive in navigating the technical complexities of autonomy.

Evolving market dynamics introduce opportunities and challenges in the maritime landscape. Market competition intensifies as more companies embrace autonomous vessels, underscoring the need for efficiency and reliability to maintain a competitive edge. Economic disparities, infrastructure development, and insurance and liability challenges are key dynamics in this evolving market. These market dynamics require resilience, adaptability, and a commitment to economic fairness.

Societal and regulatory shifts emerge as transformative forces. Public acceptance and understanding of autonomous shipping evolve as the technology becomes more commonplace. The transition of the maritime workforce, the development of ethical frameworks for autonomous decision-making, and the continuous adaptation of regulations are pivotal societal and regulatory shifts. These societal and regulatory considerations remind us that the journey into autonomy is not solely technological; it encompasses ethical, societal, and legal dimensions that require close attention and adaptation.

Chapter Ten has guided us through the shifting currents of the autonomous shipping landscape, reminding us that the future is both promising and uncertain. As the industry continues its voyage, navigating these challenges and uncertainties with innovation, adaptability, and a forward-looking spirit will be essential. The journey of autonomous shipping is one of transformation, resilience, and adaptability, and this chapter encapsulates the spirit of progress that defines the industry's evolution.

Chapter 11

RECOMMENDATIONS AND POLICY IMPLICATIONS

Chapter Eleven marks a pivotal juncture in our exploration of autonomous shipping. Here, we focus on the practical steps and policy considerations that can help shape this transformative technology's responsible, efficient, and sustainable future. This chapter outlines recommendations and policy implications that guide the adoption of autonomous ships, enhance regulatory frameworks, and encourage sustainable practices in the maritime industry.

GUIDANCE FOR AUTONOMOUS SHIP ADOPTION

The adoption of autonomous ships marks a significant transformation in the maritime industry. To navigate this uncharted territory responsibly, guidance for ship adoption is crucial. This guidance should encompass rigorous risk assessments and comprehensive planning. Shipping companies and vessel operators must conduct in-depth evaluations of potential risks associated with autonomous operations, covering safety protocols, cybersecurity measures, and compliance with legal frameworks. These assessments ensure that the adoption process is well-informed and emphasise safety at every turn.

Additionally, guidance should extend to training and workforce transition. The maritime industry should prioritise developing educational programs and reskilling initiatives, ensuring seafarers and maritime professionals can transition smoothly into roles that support autonomous ship operations. This not only safeguards the livelihoods of those involved but also leverages their invaluable expertise in ensuring the responsible adoption of autonomous technology.

Collaboration and knowledge sharing are also fundamental aspects of guidance. Encouraging stakeholders to collaborate and share best practices and lessons learned is essential for driving responsible adoption and fostering innovation. It facilitates industry-wide progress and accelerates the development of standardised procedures and protocols for autonomous operations.

Finally, guidance should stress the importance of performance monitoring and reporting. Autonomous vessel operators should establish transparent mechanisms for continuously monitoring and reporting on the performance of their fleets. These practices, in alignment with regulatory standards, help ensure the safe and efficient operation of autonomous vessels, offer insights for improvement, and contribute to the industry's commitment to responsible adoption.

REGULATORY FRAMEWORK ENHANCEMENTS

The regulatory landscape for autonomous shipping is a critical foundation for its responsible development and widespread adoption. Regulatory framework enhancements are essential in creating an environment where safety, ethics, and efficiency are paramount. First and foremost, international standardisation remains a cornerstone of regulatory progress. Collaborative efforts among nations and governing bodies are necessary to establish consistent international standards for autonomous shipping. This standardisation ensures the seamless operation of autonomous vessels across borders and fosters a shared commitment to safety and accountability on a global scale.

Ethical guidelines are a central focus of regulatory enhancements. As autonomous ships make complex decisions, developing ethical frameworks is crucial to align the technology with societal values. These guidelines help ensure that the decision-making capabilities of autonomous vessels are responsible, transparent, and ethically sound, particularly in intricate and challenging scenarios.

Liability and insurance frameworks require adaptation to the unique landscape of autonomous shipping. Regulatory bodies and the insurance industry must work in tandem to establish clear guidelines for determining liability in the event of accidents or incidents involving autonomous vessels. These guidelines provide legal clarity and accountability while addressing the complexities in a world where human operators may not always be present onboard.

Cybersecurity standards are another key aspect of regulatory framework enhancements. As autonomous vessels become more interconnected and reliant on digital technologies, stringent cybersecurity guidelines must be incorporated into regulations. These standards should continually evolve to address emerging threats and vulnerabilities, safeguarding autonomous ships against digital risks.

In this landscape of regulatory framework enhancements, the industry and its governing bodies collaborate to create an environment that encourages responsible and safe autonomous shipping. These regulatory enhancements lay the foundation for the industry's future and underscore the commitment to safety, ethics, and global cooperation in this transformative era.

ENCOURAGING SUSTAINABLE PRACTICES

Sustainability is a fundamental consideration as autonomous shipping evolves. Encouraging sustainable practices is not just an ethical imperative but also a strategic one for the industry. One of the core strategies for promoting sustainability in autonomous shipping is the reduction of emissions. Regulatory bodies and industry stakeholders should incentivise the integration of eco-friendly technologies in autonomous ships. This can encompass the use of alternative fuels, energy-efficient systems, and innovative methods to reduce the environmental footprint of maritime operations. Incentives such as tax benefits or carbon credits can motivate shipping companies to prioritise emissions reductions in their autonomous operations.

Investment in green technologies is another avenue for promoting sustainability. Policymakers and industry leaders should channel resources into research and development initiatives focusing on environmentally responsible technologies for autonomous shipping. This includes funding for projects that develop alternative fuels, energy-efficient propulsion systems, and innovative solutions for mitigating the environmental impact of maritime operations. By supporting these green initiatives, the industry demonstrates its commitment to sustainability and aligns with broader global efforts to combat climate change.

Compliance with environmental regulations is of paramount importance. Regulatory bodies should maintain and enhance existing environmental standards, ensuring autonomous ships adhere to these regulations. This includes emission limits, anti-fouling measures, and waste management practices. Stringent enforcement of these standards is essential to guarantee that sustainability remains a core focus in the industry, even as technology advances.

In encouraging sustainable practices, the maritime industry charts a path toward responsible autonomy that enhances efficiency and safeguards the environment. Sustainability in autonomous shipping is a collective responsibility driven by regulatory bodies, industry stakeholders, and a shared commitment to minimising the ecological impact of maritime operations.

Chapter 12

CONCLUSION

As we approach the concluding chapter of our exploration into the world of autonomous shipping and the pivotal role of ship management companies, it is time to reflect on the significance of the "Autonomous Wave." This concluding chapter offers a recap of the key findings, an acknowledgement of the transformational impact of autonomous shipping, and a glimpse of the continued evolution that lies ahead in the maritime industry.

RECAP OF AUTONOMOUS WAVE'S SIGNIFICANCE

The "Autonomous Wave" signifies a transformative shift in the maritime industry. Autonomous ships equipped with advanced technologies hold the promise of enhanced safety, efficiency, and cost-effectiveness. They usher in a new era where traditional practices coexist with cutting-edge autonomy, redefining how vessels operate. Autonomous ship management companies have emerged as crucial enablers of this change, providing services that range from remote monitoring and diagnostics to crew training and safety protocols.

Throughout this journey, we've explored the technologies that shape autonomous ships, the benefits they bring, and the challenges they face. We've delved into the impact of autonomy on the maritime industry, touching on the adoption of autonomous ships, the evolution of maritime jobs and skillsets, environmental benefits, and economic implications. The future of autonomous shipping, as outlined in the future trends and prospects, is marked by technological advancements, regulatory adaptation, expansion of operations, and sustainability initiatives.

OUTLOOK FOR AUTONOMOUS SHIPPING AND SHIP MANAGEMENT COMPANIES

A horizon of challenges and opportunities marks the outlook for autonomous shipping and ship management companies. With its transformative potential, autonomous shipping continues to shape the maritime industry's future. The adoption of autonomous ships is anticipated to increase, with technology rapidly evolving to enhance safety, efficiency, and sustainability. As technology matures, regulatory bodies are expected to play a more significant role in shaping the standards and ethical guidelines that govern autonomy, ensuring safe and responsible operations.

Remote monitoring, diagnostics, crew training, and safety protocols remain integral for ship management companies. Ship managers are poised to become even more crucial in facilitating the transition to autonomous operations, ensuring that the workforce adapts and vessels operate efficiently. They are at the forefront of incorporating green technologies and sustainable practices, aligning with global efforts to reduce the environmental impact of maritime operations.

A dynamic and adaptable maritime industry marks the future. Unforeseen technological challenges will emerge, demanding innovation and resilience. Evolving market dynamics will require companies to stay competitive while addressing economic disparities and promoting fairness. Societal and regulatory shifts will continue to redefine the landscape, emphasising public acceptance, ethical decision-making, and global cooperation.

In this outlook, the industry's capacity to navigate these challenges while promoting efficiency, safety, and sustainability is central. Autonomous shipping and ship management companies are not merely embracing a technological wave; they are ushering in a new era of maritime operations. The journey into autonomy is a testament to the industry's adaptability, innovation, and commitment to shaping a maritime future that is safer, more efficient, and more responsible.

RECAP OF KEY FINDINGS

Several key findings have emerged throughout this comprehensive exploration of autonomous shipping and the role of ship management companies.

First and foremost, the "Autonomous Wave" signifies a transformative shift in the maritime industry. Autonomous ships, driven by advanced technologies, promise enhanced safety, efficiency, and cost-effectiveness. The role of ship management companies is pivotal, offering services that range from remote monitoring to crew training, enabling the responsible adoption of autonomy.

The journey has unveiled the intricate technologies shaping autonomous ships, including advanced sensors, satellite navigation, AI, machine learning algorithms, and control systems. These technologies provide numerous benefits, from increased safety to operational flexibility, while introducing challenges like legal frameworks, cybersecurity concerns, and the need for trust-building with stakeholders.

The impact on the maritime industry is profound, with the increased adoption of autonomous ships, the evolution of job roles and skillsets, environmental benefits, and economic implications. Future trends suggest further technological advancements, regulatory adaptation, and sustainability initiatives.

The journey into autonomy is not solely technical but encompasses ethical and societal considerations. Public acceptance, workforce transition, and ethical decision-making represent transformative forces. Regulatory frameworks play a crucial role in creating a responsible and safe environment for autonomy, covering aspects like standardisation, ethical guidelines, liability and insurance, and cybersecurity standards.

As we conclude this exploration, the industry acknowledges the transformative impact of autonomous shipping on the maritime landscape and the global economy. The journey underscores the readiness of the industry to adapt to unforeseen challenges and continues to shape a maritime future that is autonomous, efficient, and sustainable.

ACKNOWLEDGEMENT OF AUTONOMOUS SHIPPING'S TRANSFORMATIONAL IMPACT

The acknowledgement of autonomous shipping's transformational impact is an essential reflection of the journey we've undertaken. The advent of autonomous shipping influences the maritime industry, coastal communities, and the global economy. The significance of this transformation is profound, encompassing safer, more efficient, and environmentally responsible maritime operations. Autonomous shipping has altered the very essence of how vessels operate and how the industry conducts its affairs.

As technology continues to evolve, it is imperative to recognise its power in reshaping the industry's future. It signifies not merely an adoption of advanced machinery but a fundamental shift in how we think about maritime operations. Autonomous ships represent an evolution reshaping the industry's landscape, streamlining operations, and offering potential benefits extending beyond the confines of individual vessels.

This acknowledgement carries a commitment to further exploration and adaptation. The journey is ongoing, with new challenges, opportunities, and horizons awaiting us. The transformational impact of autonomous shipping catalyses continued innovation, a commitment to ethical practices, and a shared responsibility to ensure the maritime industry remains a beacon of progress and sustainability.

In acknowledging the transformational impact of autonomous shipping, we embrace the future and underscore the industry's ability to navigate change with resilience and vision, securing a maritime landscape that is better equipped to meet the challenges of tomorrow.

A LOOK AHEAD TO THE AUTONOMOUS WAVE'S CONTINUED EVOLUTION IN MARITIME INDUSTRY

As we gaze into the horizon of the maritime industry, the continued evolution of the "Autonomous Wave" unveils a landscape marked by dynamism and adaptability. Autonomous shipping and the role of ship management companies are on a trajectory of innovation, responsiveness, and transformation.

The maritime world will witness the increased adoption of autonomous ships, driven by the ever-advancing technologies that underpin them. These vessels are expected to become more commonplace on our seas, fostering a new era where traditional practices coexist with cutting-edge autonomy. Safety and efficiency will remain paramount, and the industry's commitment to responsible adoption will be unwavering.

For ship management companies, the role is set to evolve further. Beyond remote monitoring, diagnostics, and safety protocols, these entities will become instrumental in facilitating workforce transition. The reskilling and training of maritime professionals will be a pivotal part of this evolution, ensuring that the existing workforce remains a vital and adaptable asset in the autonomous world.

Ethical considerations are likely to gain increasing prominence. As autonomous ships make complex decisions, developing ethical frameworks is crucial to align the technology with societal values. These guidelines guide responsible and transparent decision-making, especially in intricate and challenging scenarios.

Regulatory bodies will continue to play a central role in shaping the autonomous shipping landscape. The focus on international standardisation is expected to intensify, with a global commitment to establishing consistent standards that facilitate the safe and seamless operation of autonomous vessels across borders. Developing liability and insurance frameworks and strengthening cybersecurity standards will become critical aspects of regulatory adaptation.

The environmental imperative will be a driving force, with the maritime industry increasingly prioritising sustainability. Incentives for emissions reduction, investment in green technologies, and adherence to environmental regulations will guide the industry's journey towards a more environmentally responsible future.

The industry's capacity to navigate unforeseen technological challenges, evolving market dynamics, and societal and regulatory shifts will be pivotal in this evolution. The industry stands at the precipice of a transformative era, one that is not only about technological prowess but also about resilience, adaptability, and a shared commitment to shaping a maritime future that is safer, more efficient, and more responsible. As we embark on this journey, the "Autonomous Wave" propels us toward new horizons, where the maritime industry remains an enduring symbol of progress and innovation.

www.ingramcontent.com/pod-product-compliance
Lightning Source LLC
Chambersburg PA
CBHW080002130626
46546CB00014B/2775